Tom O'Toole
Breadwinner

A fresh approach to
business success from
the founder of the
Beechworth Bakery

T0342863

Tom O'Toole Breadwinner

A fresh approach to business success from the founder of the Beechworth Bakery

The must-read revised edition

With Lowell Tarling

Publishing

Published by:

Bas Publishing
ABN 30 106 181 542
PO Box 2052
Seaford Vic 3198
Tel/Fax: (03) 5988 3597
Web: www.baspublishing.com.au
Email: mail@baspublishing.com.au

Tom's website: www.tomotoole.com.au

The National Library of Australia Cataloguing-in-Publication entry

Author:	O'Toole, Tom, 1952-
Title:	Breadwinner : a fresh approach to business success from the founder of the Beechworth Bakery / Tom O'Toole with Lowell Tarling.
Edition:	New ed.
ISBN:	9781921496172 (pbk.)
Subjects:	O'Toole, Tom, 1952- Beechworth Bakery. Businessmen--Biography. Success in business. Achievement motivation.
Other Authors/ Contributors:	Tarling, Lowell.
Dewey Number:	650.1

Front image: Tom O'Toole
Back image: Tom acting as Tom

DEDICATION

To Mum and Dad

And to the unbeatable Irish spirit.

Have great hopes and dare to go all out for them. Have great dreams and dare to live them. Have tremendous expectations and believe in them.

- Norman Vincent Peale

"There are motivational coaches, there are management consultants, there are get up and go gurus everywhere but there's only one Tom O'Toole. He gets on with the job with a method and motivation, and modus operandi which can be applied way beyond his own business to almost every situation in building team spirit, making things positive and getting the job done."

- Hon. Tim Fischer (Former Deputy Prime Minister)

"Excellent... Exceeded all our expectations - hilariously fun and motivational yet filled with numerous business tips and words of wisdom. Reaches all levels. Highly recommended."

- WA Tourism Commission

"Tom's presentation was inspirational and entertaining. He captured the attention of a young group of managers and held their focus for over the hour he spoke."

- McDonalds

"Excellent. Tom's animated style in delivering his message (on how to improve business) was both insightful and hilarious - It was the tonic we needed."

- The Age

"Great story. Everybody loved him."

- National Mutual

"Extremely well received and related well to our membership base."

- Nursery Industry Association

"Tom is an inspiration. He was just the tonic we needed."

- Flinders View United Traders Association

"Personality plus. Great character. Great presentation. Excellent message. Unique style ... the highlight of the Conference."

- Retravision

"Outstanding, well presented and entertaining. He also got the right messages out."
- *Mildura Rural City Council*

"He was chosen for a purpose which he fulfilled perfectly."
- *Harvey Norman*

"Highly motivating, interesting and with many great take home messages."
- *Land and Water Conservation*

"A Super-Charged presentation."
- *United Travel Agency Group (UTAG)*

"Everyone loved Tom and learned heaps from his presentation."
- *First National Real Estate*

"All the country people want him to visit their shires to do the same for them."
- *hoo marketing pty ltd*

"His genuine enthusiasm and his unique style had even our most cynical staff hanging on his every word."
- *Casino RSL Club*

"A very strong message that everyone can receive and act upon - don't let the dreamtakers steal your dreams!"
- *Lorraine Lea Linen Pty Ltd*

"Tom's energetic and down to earth style really struck a chord with our members. A story full of impact with a ton of messages for retailers."
- *Paint Right*

"Brilliant! A true rough diamond. Fantastic. We loved him!"
- *Gelco Consulting Pty Ltd*

ACKNOWLEDGMENTS

At every moment of my life I have had people there for me. They have always made me look better than I am. Their support and encouragement made all the difference in my life. They filled my life with fun and learning. Some are all through the book – like Keith McIntosh. Others did not fit into the storyline, like: Artie and Gwen Henderson, Vern and Jan Duncan, Peter Rossetti and Barry Markoff, plus many more.

For editorial assistance I would also like to give special thanks to Robbie Tarling, Nona Toole, Betty Friar, Graeme Alford, Greg Tams, Bert Smith, Ian Hyndman, the Burke Museum (Beechworth), and my beautiful wife Christine O'Toole.

Lots of people have made my journey possible. I hope you realise how grateful I am to you.

CONTENTS

DVDs and CDs by Tom O'Toole

Making Dough With Tom O'Toole
Drop Everything For The Customer
Winning Ways
Dare to Dream

Books by Tom O'Toole

Secrets of the Beechworth Bakery (2001)
More Secrets of the Beechworth Bakery (2007)

Also by Lowell Tarling

Fiction:
Taylor's Troubles (1982)
The Secret Gang of Oomlau (1988)
1967, This Is It! (1990)
Anthologies:
All The Best, A Selection Celebrating 25 Years of Puffins In Australia (1989)
Australia's Best Poetry Vol 1 (2001)
Visions From The Valley, Poetry of the Hunter Valley 1960-2000 (2001)
Non-fiction:
Thank God For The Salvos, The Salvation Army In Australia 1880-1980 (1980)
The Edges of Seventh-day Adventism (1981)
The Australian Book of Letters (1989)
17 Small Business Success Stories (1991)
Gold Beyond Your Dreams (with Heather Turland) (1998)
No More Cellulite Fast (with Violetta Chevell) (1999)
Beyond Azaria (with Michael Chamberlain) (1999)
Brash Business (with Geoff Brash) (2000)
The Complete Tiny Tim Interviews (2000)
Breadwinner (with Tom O'Toole) (2000)
The Women's Club (with Diana Williams) (2000)
My Dad Thinks I Rob Banks (with Joe Sammon) (2001)
Risky Business (with Clare Loewenthal) (2001)
Secrets of the Beechworth Bakery (with Tom O'Toole & Matthew McLaurin) (2001)
Guilty To Driza-Bone (with Frank Fisher) (2002)
The Method, A Writer's Handbook (2002)
On The End Of A Wire (with Peter Davidson) (2004)
The Business Method (2004)
Go For Your Life! (with Chris Gray) (2005)
Busted: 17 Classic Mythbusters (2007)
South Side Story (2008)

CHAPTER ONE

GUNNER O'TOOLE

Now what's the use of worrying?
It's silly to worry, isn't it?
You're gone today and here
tomorrow.
Groucho Marx

Who the bloody hell is Tom O'Toole? I'm no big time businessman and I'm no big time public speaker either. I'm actually a kindergarten drop-out. I'm also a bit of a larrikin and a bit of a dickhead. Some people say that I've lived a remarkable life, starting as a real poor kid from Tocumwal with no education, to owning Australia's Greatest Bakery in Beechworth, Victoria.

For me to write a book is terrifying because I don't like sticking myself right out there. I can't imagine my face in a bookshop. I mean, *who the bloody hell is Tom O'Toole?* Who's going to read a book about me? Friends said: "Tom, your grammar's not good enough, you have no schooling. They're gonna think you're a real bloody clown after they read this!" So I had to tone my swearing down a lot.

Why write a book? Well it wasn't my bloody idea I can tell you. This mad publisher and his bloody writer wanted me to write it and I said, "Geez I dunno" and it went in the too-hard basket. It was terrifying to think about this book because I'm like everybody else, I've got skeletons in the cupboards and I don't want them to come out and bite me on the bum.

Then I started saying, I was 'gunner' do it. I was gunner write the book. I was gunner, gunner, gunner. I'm a real good gunner, I should have been in the Army.

Then I thought, I want to do the best job I possibly can. So I got right into it.

I've tried hard to be factual and to put my story together correctly, but it's still not perfect. It's still not smooth. I hope I haven't offended anyone. I know for a fact that I've left people out, but then again - you can't put everyone and everything in.

LET'S GET STARTED

Now that I've said that, let's get started. This book is about making dough, the paper sort of dough. It will hopefully get you out of your comfort zone, it certainly got me out of mine.

To make it better for you – so you can see where I'm coming from – I've listed seven key philosophies in this chapter, but that's just to give you a taste of what's to come. I want you to lend an ear – persevere - give a cheer. I want you to read the whole book.

Nothing I say is original, but then again, what is? Probably some is. Some of it is my life and that's *got* to be original. Sometimes I pinch or Australianise other people's ideas. But I'm no big time guru.

However, over the years I felt it was important to write down my goals, and while I had a pen in my hand I also jotted down the essence of what I learned through reading and living. This turned out to be a fair wad of handwritten pages, but I sorted them out, and that became the guts of my business ideas. I hope you enjoy them.

I know I can't please everybody, so I don't usually try. In fact, trying to please everyone is a good recipe for going broke.

I can't please all my staff, I can't please all my customers, now here I am worrying about pleasing a group of people I never thought I'd have to worry about – you lot!

WELCOME TO BEECHWORTH

If you're going to Beechworth you're going out of your bloody way. It's not on the road to the snowfields, it's not on the road to Wangaratta, it's not on the road to Albury, it was by-passed 100 bloody years ago.

Today people say: "Geez, wasn't Beechworth smart saving all its heritage and its history." It wasn't the bloody smartness of the town, it was the bloody poverty. No one would spend any money on the town, it was slowly dying. Today it's very much a tourist town, but it's still on a road to nowhere.

In 1984, when I bought the Beechworth Bakery for the second time, people didn't say, "I'm going for a drive to Beechworth" unless they were going to visit Mad Auntie in the lunatic asylum, or one of their relations in the jail. Back then it was a Government town, not so much a tourist town.

Tourists tended to go for a drive to Bright, a beautiful town, on the Ovens River, 50 minutes away. Still, nobody said, "I'm going for a drive to Beechworth" because if you're going to Beechworth, you're going out of your bloody way.

Today, it's one of the premier tourist destinations in north-east Victoria. There's lots of reasons for that: one is the Beechworth Bakery, another is the historical importance of the town and its architecture. And, of course, there are other reasons too, like the Powder Magazine (built in the 1850s), the historic precinct, the

Chinese Burning Towers and the Court House where Ned Kelly and his mother Ellen were tried.

This is the town that has given me everything I have: my family, my business, my home and my reputation. It is also the town where I found both the time and the need to sit back, take a look at business, take a look at life and try to figure out what it's all about.

And I have concluded that it's about getting up in the morning, *in love with life and rarin' to go!*

Here are seven ways to *git into it!*

1. BEWARE THE DREAM-TAKERS

One of the main messages of this book is: "Beware The Dream-Takers." It would have made a good title.

There's heaps of dream-takers who'll tell you it can't be done. Our mates, bank managers, accountants, even our partners say, "You're not going to live long enough! That's too big a dream!"

Well, at least try.

Beware the dream-takers, they're like bloody mosquitoes, they're everywhere.

I'm hoping this book gets you in contact with your dreams. Most of us go into business with big aspirations and in time we forget what they were. My business was once my life – today my business gives me a life.

My staff says, "Tom we should do this, we should do that" and I say, "No, bugger off!" because I can be a dream-taker too. We are our own worst enemies – always, always! We don't need any other enemies when we've got our bloody selves. We think it's too hard, we think it takes too long! I've got to be really *really* careful with my kids that I don't steal their dreams.

I want to be a dream-giver.

When I was a kid, I sure liked to dream. I'd be pushing the mower around Father Byrne's lawn, thinking and thinking at a million miles an hour about what I wanted to do with my life. At first, money was my main motivation – because my family didn't have any. Much later in life I learned that Father Byrne had found a peace within himself that I didn't have – no matter how much money I was making. And so I had to find a mirror and take a hard look at myself. I think Father Byrne would be fairly proud of me if he met me now. Today I am a public speaker. I talk to many diverse groups, including CEOs and professional bodies, yet for Father Byrne I'd bring water instead of wine, I'd drop things, I'd giggle in prayer. My first words in public were as an altar boy, and I buggered them right up.

2. WHAT ARE YOU FAMOUS FOR?

What are you famous for? I have to ask myself that question every day: "What are we famous for?"

What is it about the Beechworth Bakery? Is it our freshness? Is it our staff? Is it our town? Is it our Pyjama Days? Is it our building? Is it our product? Is it me?

It's a perception really. I simply tell people we're famous, and I use the expression, "The Famous Beechworth Bakery". You tell 'em often enough, and they believe you.

But, *what are we famous for Tom? What are we famous for?*

Most businesses are not famous at all. But if we're not famous, I get agitated and think: "Shit, we've got to get famous for something!"

What are *YOU* famous for?

You've got to be famous for something.

3. GET OUT OF YOUR COMFORT ZONE

In 1999 I was at a conference in New Zealand and bungee jumping was one of the activities on offer.

Everyone said: "Come on Tom, you're always talking about getting us out of our comfort zone, we want to see you get out of yours!" They were ragging me a bit, then someone said: "Are you gunner to jump or not?"

"No way," I replied. (Talking the talk is very easy for me, but *walking the talk* ah, that's a different story.)

But then I felt that to be honest with myself, I had to have a go. Here I was preaching that everyone else should get out of their comfort zones but I wasn't prepared to do it myself. If I'd thought too much about it, I know I'd never have done the jump, but I whacked the brain into neutral and bought a ticket. It cost me a lot of bloody money to try to kill myself!

My wife Christine was horrified when she realised what was going on. She wasn't very impressed that I was going to do this bungee jump.

I went out on the platform and the instructor said, "Is this your first time?" Well, he could see it was my first time, I couldn't even bloody speak! So they trussed me up.

Christine was watching all this in a semi-state of shock. "What if you lose your teeth?" she yelled. That's what she was concerned about, not the rest of my body! So just before the jump I said to an instructor, "Will I lose me teeth?" He thought that was funny and repeated it to the other instructor. They'd never heard a line like that before.

And so I jumped off and for the first few moments it was a terrifying experience. When the rope took up the slack, I felt a great surge of excitement that – wow! – I had actually made the leap. Then I relaxed and I began to see a whole new perspective on the world. My whole life was in front of me and the horizon was so far away. It took me way back…

When I was a young boy I was fishing with my brother Mickey. We were sitting on a fallen tree in the Murray River. It had been there for months. All of a sudden the entire trunk rolled over and we were sucked under water. Twisting and turning among the branches, I thought, "This is the end, I'm going to drown". My whole life flashed before my eyes - and then I scrambled out of the branches and swam to the top. Mickey had done the same.

That was an awakening of sorts, for me on that log. And this bungee jumping was the same thing. When I jumped, it made me question all sorts of life and death values.

I don't like getting out of my comfort zone, but if I'm out there telling people they've got to get out of theirs, I've got to get out of mine. I've got to walk the talk and jump the jumps.

4. TAKE A RISK – SMILE!

Everything you want is just outside your comfort zone. One of the things I say to people is: "Take a risk – smile! – live! Don't just exist – live! The person who does not take a risk has nothing, is nothing, becomes nothing. Only the person who risks is truly free."

Ask yourself: "How long am I going to be dead?" You're going to be dead a long, long time. So take a bloody risk and enjoy life. It's easy to exist, but it takes a bit of effort to really live. I wouldn't be dead for quids.

Most weeks I go into the local Beechworth Jail and I talk to the prisoners. I often ask the guys: "Where do *you* want to be in five years?"

Well, some of them are still going to be in jail – others are planning to turn their lives around. But they're all great at blaming somebody else for their troubles. I too was a great blamer, but I've learned that it doesn't matter what our past has been, we all have a clean future: *yesterday's history and tomorrow's a mystery.* It's that simple.

Every day is a fresh one, and it's ready for you to fill with excitement.

When I tell people to take a risk, to get enthusiastic, to fall in love with life, to get going, some of them turn to me and say: "I'll do it when I'm organised...."

Bull shit! Tomorrow's success begins today! Don't wait until you're bloody organised! You're never gonna be organised!

If you wait, you'll be saying: "When my kids get a bit bigger, I'm going to travel around Australia."

A couple of years later it's: "When the kids finish high school, then I'll travel."

And after that: "When they finish uni...."

And finally: "When my grandkids get a little bit bigger, I'll...."

Then you're dead!

Don't wait until you're organised. The secret of getting ahead is getting started. When are you going to be organised? Two years? Five years?

It's all crap! You're either gonna to do it or you're not. Everyone is waiting for something to happen. And everybody is waiting for someone else to do it.

Nothing changes if nothing changes. Action is a magic word. Before anything will change, I've got to change. *If it's to be, it's up to me* - what a pain in the bum, because I wanted it to be up to someone else!

```
When we were little I was told,
  be careful, be careful Tommy,
We start walking, be careful, be careful,
```

We get on our push bike,
be careful, be careful,
We start going to school, be careful
crossing the road, be careful,
We get our car licence we're told,
be careful, be careful,
We get our girlfriend, we're told
to **be careful, be extra careful**,
We get our own businesses, we're
told, be careful, be careful,
Everyone tells you to be careful.
No one tells you:
take risks Tommy,
Take risks.
I've taken a big risk
writing this bloody book.
It's a risk for some of youse to smile.
If you're bloody happy,
tell your face.
Smile.

5. ENJOY YOUR WORK

Hey you! We all spend a lot of time working - so we might as well enjoy the experience - and the only way to do that is to be positive and enthusiastic about everything you do. If your heart's in it, the sky's the limit. Get in there boots 'n' all. If you're not happy, change – or get out. Why waste a day of your life doing something you don't like doing, and there's so many people out there wasting their lives doing stuff they hate.

Making an honest crust isn't pie in the sky.

Being a baker is not a gravy train.

In fact, being a baker goes against the grain.

It's a bit of a bun fight and it's bloody hard work.

But then again what work isn't hard? Physical work is hard enough, but I reckon it's even harder when you're using your brain. So beat it with enthusiasm. Don't go saying, "It's hard!

It's hard!

It's hard!

It's hard!

It's hard!

It's hard!"

Being prepared to work hard opened many doors for me. Nothing worthwhile is ever achieved without that collective spark of enthusiasm. If you're not getting what you want out of life, check your level of enthusiasm.

To become enthusiastic, just act enthusiastic – that's how simple it is! *Fake it 'til you make it* (like your partner does!).

If you can't be enthusiastic, just fake it. Brag! Take a risk! Fake a risk! Hey, if you're doing a worthwhile job it has got to be braggable! I tell my staff, "Get enthusiastic! Talk up the business. Have a belief in the product, have a belief in the community, have a belief in yourselves, for I know the believers in this life pick up the prizes." Enjoy your work. Enjoy your family. Live life to the full. Always ask yourself, "How long am I going to be dead?"

Sometimes you can be a bit too enthusiastic! I was so enthusiastic I stuck my hand in a moulder – but I'll get to that later. I was so enthusiastic I wore kneepads to strengthen my knees, because I was spending so much time on my legs. Another time I was moulding so much bread that I was getting cortisone injections to kill the pain and to keep me going. The doctor gave me three cortisone injections into my elbows over a short period of time, then said:

"Tom, I can't give you no more." But I couldn't stop working. Sometimes I'm a bit too positive. I'm no bloody role model.

But today, I know I've got to enjoy my life. So I talk up my work all the time. I've gotta tell myself I love baking. Bloody hell, if I'm getting out of bed at 3 am, I've *got* to tell myself I love baking! That self-talk is so important to me - especially at three in the morning – because I understand that I only have one day to enjoy, and that's *today.*

Yesterday

with all its aches and mistakes and
regrets and remorse and guilt,
it's gone forever.

You can't do a bloody thing about
yesterday. It's history.

And tomorrow's a mystery, the sun
will rise either behind a mask of
clouds or in a ray of sunshine.

Until it does you have no
stake in tomorrow at all.

So that only leaves you today.

Any one can get through the
battles of one day.

It's only when you join yesterday
and tomorrow together

– that's when you go mad.

I know

I've been there.

Live every day as if it's your last and
one day you're gonna be right.

6. HAVE GOALS

Most people don't have any bloody goals!

The most important thing about goals is *having one.* The next most important thing is having them on paper. When I started to write down my goals, and date them, it changed my life dramatically.

My wife won't write any goals on paper. She's like the rest of youse.

I believe if your goals are not on paper, they're not on this planet. For me, they've got to be written because I've got this big empty black hole in my head where nothing sticks around for long. It's easy to fire a bullet in any direction and claim that whatever it hit was your target. It's easy to change direction or make it up as you go along if it's only in your head - but if it's on paper, it's captured.

I've got to have goals.

If I haven't got goals - what am I doing it all for?

I've got to have *big* goals!

I set big goals,

I set little goals,

I set achievable goals,

I set goals that I've really got to stretch for,

I set goals I've really got to go hard for.

I set goals.

Goals are just dreams with a date, that's all they are. And we must all dream.

And although I'm one of the main creative ideas people at the Beechworth Bakery, anyone is entitled to dream up anything. Thinking is allowed. We encourage everyone to have a go.

I want to go down the Murray River in a bathtub. (Goal achieved January 2005)

I've still got lots of dreams and lots of goals.

I want to take my story all over the world.

7. SHOCK PEOPLE

Live a bigger life!

Do things with your life!

Get an idea!

Get motivated!

Get going!

Surprise people!

Shock people!

Just do it!

For example, try pleasing your staff, even if it frightens them at first.

It'll frighten *you* at first. I must admit it unsettled me.

Also try pleasing your bloody partner even if it frightens them! If I did the dishes, it'd terrify my wife Christine. She'd think, "What's he been up to?" So I sometimes do the dishes, as well as my usual job of taking out the chook bucket.

Force yourself to take the initiative – *do things*. Take a look at your business – and your life – with fresh eyes. It's really hard to do that because we get so comfortable. We become town-blind, community-blind and store-blind. Ideas have got to come from somewhere, and for me to get that vision, I've got to go *beyond* my own backyard. That's not the only place where you'll find ideas that shock and excite people; sometimes they're right under our noses, but we can't always see them because we're too complacent and comfortable.

I've been going overseas regularly since I was 21. Like bungee jumping and nearly drowning, it gets me right out of my comfort zone and I'm able to come back and look at my business in a new light. I take at least two – sometimes three – holidays a year, because I like to get that fresh angle.

I believe you've got to go beyond your own barby, which is why I send my staff to other bakeries, overseas and in Australia. I want them to experience a constant stream of fresh ideas. I want them to get that vision too. Helen Keller said, "Worse than being blind is to see but have no vision".

But if time or money makes travel prohibitive, a book will always take you beyond your own horizons. Reading certainly changed my life; it shocked me into entering a new world of positive ideas, and I used to be Mr Negative, Mr Defeatist, Mr Poor Poor Pitiful Me. I used to hold pity-parties all by myself and then – *and then* – I read a book by Norman Vincent Peale. Did that shock me into positive thought? Wow, it was bloody incredible!

```
     I've got to shock myself as well as
                other people.
    My staff often needs a bloody shock.
    One of my aunties had electric shock
                 treatment.
     It got her right out of her comfort
                    zone.
            Maybe I need it too.
```

I'M A SHOCKER

There were 360 people in the hall. I had just done a talk and it was Question Time. A guy stood up and told me how his staff wasn't motivated, how they couldn't do this and they wouldn't do that. I said: "Hold on, hold on, have a look in the mirror, you'll see what the problem is."

It was a bit rough. But anyway, it stopped the questions.

He came up to me afterwards and he liked what I'd said – so that was okay. Any time I've got problems in my business, I know I've got to look at *me*. I'm just like him: I had to get a mirror that worked. For years there was no one looking back at me from that mirror. Just a blurred image of an unhappy successful businessman who wouldn't stand still for long and who had very little self-discipline and broken dreams.

And so I started dreaming. I had ideas for a second, a third, even a fourth Beechworth Bakery. It was a big dream because our bakeries are very capital intensive. I didn't want to have hundreds of them, just a few. I wrote that goal down and dated it. Today the Beechworth Bakery is expanding in ways I could never have imagined, we now have six locations in Victoria.

NEW HORIZONS

When I was at a Bakery Conference in Germany I was told this bloody good joke by a New Zealand baker. He said: "Tom, how do you tell when an Australian is on the level?"

I said: "I don't know, how?"

He said: "When the dribble's coming out both sides of his mouth."

That's a question I've got to constantly ask myself: is the dribble coming out?

I can waffle on and waffle on about my life, my bakery, my ideas, but is that what you need to know? Here's a recommendation when you read this book:

take

what

you

want

and

leave

the

rest.

Some people say, "It's okay for him, he's in the dough" – the bloody white dough – but the paper dough is what it's all about. Baking is a hard game, very labour intensive, if you pick a business where you use your brain (law, accountancy, politics, organised crime) you can make a lot more bloody money. But that's okay, because nowadays I'm in both types of dough, and I'm happy with life.

I'm happily married today. I have four kids and lots of grandkids who love me and I love them, and I can tell them I love them. That's wonderful.

Now I've also got a speaking career.

But it's much easier being in the bakehouse, because I'm no polished public speaker.

I had to do a talk to a group in Western Australia. To be a part of this audience your company had to turn over in excess of $US20 million pa. Some of these CEOs own the whole bloody company and they got *me* - a bloody kindergarten drop-out - as their guest speaker!

I said to them: "You've got the wrong man!"

They said: "No, no, you've been recommended."

So I get to talk to all different groups. Sometimes I talk to Information Technology (IT) groups! Bloody hell! I'm yet to use a calculator! But I talk to them about human nature – and that's what a business is. Even IT companies need humans to run the business. The fundamentals don't change. Bussiness is mostly about people.

Believe me, being a public speaker is right out of my comfort zone. I don't advertise, though on my business card I've now got 'Tom O'Toole - Baker and Inspirational Speaker'. (Some people call me a 'motivational' speaker, but I'm no 'motivational' speaker. Talk to my kids - I can't even motivate them to clean their rooms.)

So that's what this book is trying to do, inspire you as well as giving you a different perspective on your life. Plus, it's an easy read.

Most of our lives are full of sacred cows. We get so rutted in our ways that we work the same way from Monday to Friday, we sit in the same chair every day and we sleep on the same side of the bed every night. It's incredible how we get so set in our ways. But we've got to break that cycle - and the day I did that bungee jump, I saw new horizons.

This book, hopefully, will do the same for you.

Although I won't have it said that I'm a 'motivational' speaker, maybe I am a bit inspirational, because a lot of people think, "If this bugger can make it in business, *anyone* can".

Who the bloody hell is Tom O'Toole?

Let's find out.

CHAPTER TWO

THE TOCUMWAL KID

The local legend claimed that by the township of Tocumwal there was a hole in the river which was bottomless, and also an underground stream which ran to The Rock, seven miles away.

A. W. Reed, Aboriginal Words and Place Names

When I grew up in Tocumwal, Albury and Shepparton were 'the big smoke', I never even knew where Albury was. So you city folk have got to do a big turnaround in your thinking if you want to understand this chapter.

When I was growung up, Tocumwal was a quiet border town on the New South Wales side of the Murray River. It's on the Newell Highway, 736km south-west of Sydney and 257km north of Melbourne. The countryside is real flat, which was the attraction during the Second World War when the US Air Force built the biggest aerodrome in the Southern Hemisphere in Toc.

31

When I was born there in 1952, its population was about 2000.

By the time I was racing around the town, the War Hospital was long gone; I never saw it. It stood where they now graze sheep and cattle. When I was a kid, Tocumwal was a dry place with mostly dirt roads. The Murray River is lined with River Red gums, smooth, mottled, buff and grey. We played and we lived on that river. And every year someone would drown in it.

Toc was a town that wasn't going anywhere. Everywhere you looked, you'd see it dying. Closing the aerodrome and 'pulling out of Toc' was the big activity when I was a kid. I remember seeing the war planes flying in to get de-commissioned. Those planes were cut up then trucked out in pieces to the smelters. After the post-war effort, everything in town slowed right down and the work dropped off.

The Terminus Hotel, Merrington's Newsagency, Haines' Butchery and the water tower are still around today. But the old fawn-coloured Flour Mill is now derelict; it used to be a real structure in the town. And I also remember the Tip, where we used to look for treasures and bottles. That was our territory. By pushbike and by foot we would roam the scrub where the massive Tocumwal Golf Course is today. Other times we would hang around the cemetery. But the best place of all was the river. It was 'our place'. Some people might be comfortable in shopping arcades, but we loved the Murray.

I often look at the river for inspiration. The river has both the strength and the tranquillity I love.

THE RIVER

Today the Murray River is dying – it's running backwards - well, it's hardly running at all, low in the summer and lower in the winter, and it's full of European carp. But when I was a kid it was very proud and powerful. And I remember staring at that beautiful river snaking past and always at peace with itself.

It was summer and I was standing with my mate Kevin Dale, near the woodheap at home, looking at the river through the gum trees. Watching, watching, watching the river flowing. We were only young and we were talking about what was happening in our lives.

I had no doubts that I was going to be a success. I had this Irish 'knowing'. I told him, "I'm going to go into business."

And Kevin knew that I had this knowing, and he was amazed. He said: "You bloody will too, you bugger! I know you will!" He reinforced my belief in myself. **WOW!** It must have sounded like a real fantasy, standing beside the woodheap that day.

When I'm at the dentist's or anywhere like that – that's where I put my mind today. On the river is where I go for my peace.

TOCUMWAL BRIDGE

Beyond the railway station is the famous Tocumwal Bridge, but we called it the 'Red Bridge'. It was opened in March 1895 and modified in 1908 to carry rail traffic. This marked the start of Tocumwal as an important railway town. All the border rail and road traffic used it to cross states.

The Red Bridge made a dramatic impact on the economy because for the first time Riverina primary producers could sell directly into Victoria. It made a huge impact on our lives, too. It was one of the best places to catch crayfish. Nowadays there's a new road to Melbourne which virtually by-passes the town, and the trains are seldom used in Toc - though when I was a kid, the only way into Victoria from Toc, was across that bridge.

We often swam at the Red Bridge, though it was quite dangerous because of the current. It was where people would go to commit suicide. It had a sort of dark mystic quality. It was deep water and we'd often dive off the bridge. It was 'the other kids' swimming hole', not 'the Toole's swimming hole'.

In terms of impacting on our lives, the Bridge and the railway created an atmosphere that something was 'happening' in Toc, when really nothing was happening at all.

TOOLE

My Dad, Christopher Toole, is Irish. Yes, that's 'Toole', not 'O'Toole'.

My parents were both known as 'Tooley'. It's what Mum would call Dad, and what the neighbours called either Mum or Dad. As for me, my bloody nicknames were 'Shovel' and 'Dickhead'. And sometimes 'Turtle' – because I was a bit slow.

Toole is a great Irish family. My ancestors fought in the 1798 Rising against the British in Wicklow, and my Toole ancesters Thomas, Patrick, Andrew, James and Philip are buried in the nave of the ruined church at Glendalough in Wicklow. Again, in 1798 some Tooles fought with the United Irishmen at Dunshaughlin, but they were defeated.

With a background like that, no wonder my father got himself into trouble. He joined the Irish Army, fought against the English and was jailed. When he got out, his relations said to him, "We're not having a jailbird here" and so my father came to Australia. His family thought they would never see him again because 'all the savages would eat him'. But that didn't stop them letting him go off to another hemisphere.

Back in Ireland, my father's parents were poor farmers. Mum always told us that there was some fabulous wealth somewhere in our family tree, way, way back, but we never believed her and neither did Dad. His parents, James Toole and Katy (née Fitzsimons), are buried in the Ratoath Cemetery, not far from Dublin, and if you want to find a lot of Tooles – go to Ratoath: I did.

In 1983, I hopped off the plane in Ireland, hired a car, and drove until I came to the little town of Ratoath where there was a real estate sign proclaiming 'Toole & Mackay'. I thought, "This is it!" so I went into the pub and asked: "Do you know where the Tooles are?" And they said, "They're all bloody here. This is the last place God built and he left all his Tooles here" – and I laughed. They all laughed too.

When I met my Father's elderly cousins they asked: "Does he still recite poetry? He sure did as a kid!"

MUM & DAD'S BACKGROUND

My Dad was in Australia during the Second World War, working as a civilian driver at the airfield. He also worked as a horseman and a rabbiter in north New South Wales and Queensland.

Mum's father, Tom Saunders, was a farmer who drowned in the Murray River, near Howlong. Today I have 100 acres not far from where he drowned. But I never met him.

My father Christopher met Nona Saunders, my Australian-born mother, in Yarrawonga, in a café where she worked. Later in life I bought my first business in Yarrawonga, the Victorian town located on Lake Mulwala.

"Tooley and I were good readers," says Mum, who was 17 years younger than Dad. "Tooley used to recite poems – Henry Lawson, Banjo Patterson – not so much the Irish poets. When he came out to Australia, he worked on the stations all around Queensland and, of course, the thing to do was to read poetry books. You couldn't get the newspapers way out where he was. Between Nyngen and Bourke there's a big pipeline, and Tooley helped build it. Times weren't too bloody easy. Tooley was working for Shimmy MacDonald, and when the war started they took away Shimmy's trucks and everybody had to go to St Marys in Sydney until they all got sacked. Then they ended up at Mulwala, where he worked in the explosives factory. I worked in the Mayfair Café and he used to come in for his meals. What attracted me to Tooley? I'm buggered if I know. I didn't understand his accent. I didn't even know if I was saying 'yes' or 'no' in the right places."

Mum used to be a regular churchgoer. She was baptised three times, first by the Church of England, then by the Church of Christ, then by the Catholic Church to fit in with Dad. The Saunders side of the family wasn't too happy when Mum married a Catholic, so we never had much to do with them in the early days.

Mum started attending the Catholic Church in Yarrawonga where she couldn't see eye to eye with the old priest. Fortunately, Dad suddenly said: "Right-io, you're coming back to Toc, I've got a room for you."

Mum came to Toc and stayed with Mrs Jeans, mother of Allan Jeans the famous AFL footballer and coach. Jeans, who played 77 games for St Kilda (1955-1959) caught St Kilda's eye on the Tocumwal Oval. Mum boarded with the Jeans family when Allan was still going to school.

MEET THE FAMILY

When I was born, our home was an Army tent with lino on the dirt floor. A lot of people lived in tents in Tocumwal during the war and even though those days had come and gone, we were still living in a tent with a cement sheeted kitchen which had a timber floor until the white ants ate it. Then we pulled it all up and went back to the lino covered dirt floor. Our home in Tuppal Street, Tocumwal didn't have a lot of things. Our acre and a half block didn't even have a bloody number.

Dad was 44 when I was born. I was the second youngest. My brother James is 11 months three weeks younger, so we are both twins for a week. Mum always told us we were both mistakes.

I remember Dad as a casual labourer on the railways. He was never permanent, which meant that every time the railways went on strike or when they didn't have enough work, Dad was laid off. Not being permanent also meant Dad never had proper documents. He never even got around to putting in a tax return. Later in life, when he went to get a pension, he couldn't get it because he didn't have any documents. He had to write to Ireland to get his birth certificate, and he found out he was a year older than he thought and had been celebrating his birthday in the wrong month.

I have one sister and three brothers. Here they are, from oldest to youngest:

1. Mickey. Mickey is seven years older than me. He likes to be known as 'Mad Mick' now, but his real nickname was 'Turtle'. He thought he copped the nickname because he caught turtles, but it was really because Mick and I are a bit slow. One time Mickey peppered James with sparrow shot. Mum picked pellets out of James for days. I hit him over the head with a broom once and smashed the broom. Mum was upset (about the busted broom).

2. Betty. Betty is five years older than me. She was tidy, bossy and very, very sensible. She would discipline us and go crook. Betty was different because she was a girl and we were smelly boys. One night I chucked a stone which hit her in the middle of the head and knocked her over. She never knew it was me. I never said a word.

3. Terry. Terry is three years older than me. He was placid, mild and sometimes a bit dramatic - but we were all a bit dramatic. One day I was going to shoot him. I had him aimed up right between the bloody eyes, but the gun wouldn't go off because there was a spent shell in the breech.

4. Me. Mickey tried to kill me with a big rock. Terry has shot me. Betty didn't try to kill anybody and neither did James. James didn't even try to get his own back when Mickey blasted him with sparrow shot.

5. James. James is a gentle person, and one day I pulled out a bottle of petrol and said to James: "Do you want a drink of plonk?" He said: "Yes." He grabbed it, took two big gulps and went off his head. He raced around the house like a blowfly. He couldn't breathe. In the end he stuck his head in the fish pond. Mum said: "What's wrong? What's wrong?" I said: "He swallowed an apricot stone."

I had a happy childhood.

Nowadays, Mickey lives in Mount Isa, Betty lives in Beechworth, Terry lives in Tocumwal. And James lives in Beechworth and works in the Post Office opposite the bakery.

The only other person on our block was a quiet old man called Youngie. He lived for a time in the chookshed which was made out of flattened four gallon drums. That wasn't so unusual either. Tocumwal was on the swaggie route.

ON THE SWAGGIE TRAIL

The swaggies were a real part of our childhood; there were always swaggies to talk to. They came through nearly every week, because we lived on the river. Some were friendly, others weren't real nice. We'd often sit around their camp fires, talking to them. They told us stories – about the cities, about life.

But we were terrible buggers. Sometimes, if we had a few bullets, when no one was watching we'd chuck them in their camp fire and then head home, knowing they were going to explode soon. It wasn't a very nice thing to do, but then again the swaggies weren't always nice either. We'd stir some of them up and they'd bloody throw sticks at us, but they weren't usually a problem. Most of the time they were good fun.

RAAF STATION

Sometimes we played on the great spits of sand along the Murray River; other times we hung around the largest RAAF station in the country. The RAAF was still dismantling the Spitfires, Lancaster bombers and the World War II hardware, and carting everything away. They would chuck hundreds of machine guns in the dams, and me and my brothers would nick in there (because you'd have to hide) and we would search for brass shells and lead bullets which we would sell off as scrap metal.

Every now and then the Police would come to our school and tell us 'don't touch ' if we found hand grenades, bullets or bombs. Of course we did. It was common to find them especially when we were digging for worms. We'd often dig up big shells, bombs or explosives in the garden, the chook yard or in the lagoons.

PRIMARY SCHOOL

I went to the Sacred Heart Primary School, 3km away but in the same street as our home. The school oval seemed so huge when I was a kid.

I hated school with a passion. My Mum and Dad couldn't afford to pay the 10 shillings a week per child to attend the school, so in return for our attendance fee, my parents provided produce. Every Sunday we took a chook to the convent and the nuns had that chook for dinner. Now *we* didn't have chook for dinner every Sunday!

My parents also kept the convent in eggs and vegetables. I couldn't understand why all our best food would go to other people, yet Mum always put it aside and never thought about touching it. She'd say: "What you don't have, you don't miss." While the nuns ate our chook, we were fed bloody pigeons, galahs, rabbits, fish, white cockies, anything!

After the RAAF pulled out, Tocumwal became a poor town. Although I had a happy childhood, I really hated living in poverty. I hated wearing other people's hand-me-downs. For example, my first pair of shoes were a pair of wool-lined nun's shoes. When the soles wore out, we would put cardboard in the shoes to stop water getting in. Lots of people in our town did the same. Not many people had cars – they couldn't afford them. If you got a ride to church in a car when I was a young boy – wow!

I failed kindergarten. I didn't learn a thing at school. I never learned the alphabet. In arithmetic, I got as far as the two-times table. The nuns belted the shit out of me, but I deserved it. I was such a pain in the arse that I spent a lot of time being locked up in a cupboard underneath the blackboard. They stuck me in this cupboard and I loved it! They also locked me up in tool shed when I got a bit bigger. It became the Toole shed.

I loved being locked up in the cupboard. I also loved being locked up in the shed instead of going to class. I often like to isolate myself today; I get into my study and I love it.

I wouldn't like being locked up in jail though. I wouldn't like that at all because you're in there with other people.

I would do crazy things in class, like suddenly running across the desktops, jumping out the window and running away. I did that more than once. The Catholic school backs onto a creek which feeds into the Murray River. I'd cross the creek, run past the peppercorn trees, race past the big prickle bushes, and try to make it home. But the nuns would send four kids after me – and they'd always catch me. They'd pick me up, one on each arm and one on each leg, then they'd carry or drag me back.

When I got into the bigger classes, I couldn't do the work. The teacher would say: "Tom, who discovered Australia?"

I'd say: "You dunno, do you?"

"Why'd you say that?"

I'd reply: "If you knew, you wouldn't ask me!" *Ha ha.*

I had an attitude problem. I could never get in step. I wagged heaps of school, I pinched boats. Like Huck Finn, I just messed about on the river.

People now say to me: "Tom, you must've been dyslexic...." I dunno, I was just told I was dumb. I read now, but I never did then, though my kids are real readers.

A few years ago, I told the press that I don't know the alphabet and Mum read that interview. She said: "Tom, you know what? I don't know the ABC either!" However she was a good reader, but Mum couldn't write much. She wrote like a grade 3 person, which was great for me, because that meant I could write the note myself when I wagged school. The nun would read: "Tom is sick today, N. Toole," and it'd be my handwriting – meanwhile I'd be down the river, pinching boats or building forts.

Even walking to school was unpleasant. We had to go past the Tocumwal State School where kids hung out at the fence. When they'd see us they'd chant, *Catholic dogs, Sitting on logs, Eating maggots, Out of frogs.*

I've never been to a school reunion, but now that those painful days seem like fun, I probably would if they invited me. I'm too big to fit in the cupboard now.

HOME SWEET HOME

As a kid I couldn't work out why we had rips in our walls – I didn't really realise it was a tent. A kid doesn't go: "Oh we live in a *brick veneer house*" or "We live in a *weatherboard home.*" It's just home. When the canvas started to rot Dad started putting cement sheets over it.

We had a cement sheeting kitchen and an outside pan dunny. When I left home at 16 we still didn't have the sewerage. I was 28 when Mum and Dad got the sewerage put on. We were the last house in Toc to get off the pan.

One day the health inspector showed up, checked out our living conditions and said: "You've got to get a bigger place." That's when we stopped living in the tent. When I was seven years old, an old one-bedroom, four-room house was moved by truck onto our block. Dad built two extra bedrooms on the end of the house with leftover RAAF timber. Within the first month we broke every window in the place. The tent didn't have windows, and we didn't realise we couldn't throw stones inside a house without busting things. After 30 years, my brother Terry eventually repaired all the windows. Mum lived in that pastel green weatherboard cottage until it burned down in 2005.

We didn't have electricity for many years, we didn't have a sink and we didn't have appliances. We used a Coolgardie safe until Mickey bought our first refrigerator for 10 quid – my parents made him buy it, which he wasn't too bloody pleased about. He still complains about it, and that was 40 years ago.

We never really had a bathroom until I was nine, and then when we did get a bath, the water wasn't connected until years later. We used to carry the water by bucket or sometimes we'd stick the hose through the louvred windows. At school I'd stink, and the nuns would try to wash me, but I was a bad-tempered bastard and I'd wouldn't let them touch me. I'd go down the river and wash there instead. When we got older we'd nick up to the railway station and have a shower. We'd sleep in our unwashed clothes and at times we'd pee the bed. My Mum didn't change the sheets very often – so we'd just piss the bed again. Sometimes the nuns would wash our clothes.

In fact, our sleeping quarters weren't too great. Betty had a room to herself but we four boys crammed into a 12' x 10' room. It had one window, and three single beds. I slept in the same bed as my brother James until the age of 11 when I set a goal that I was going to buy a double bunk. I pinned the picture of the bed I wanted on my wall, and I left it there until I got it. It was the first major goal I ever achieved. I learned early in life that goal-setting works.

DOUBLE-BUNK BREAKTHROUGH

I can remember flicking through a catalogue and there I saw it: a basic chrome double bunk. *Wow, the thing I wanted most!* I had been sleeping with my younger brother all my life and I hated it. He'd fart so much, or maybe it was me, but oh, it wasn't much fun. One of us'd pee the bed and we didn't know which one. I know I was a bed wetter and I'm sure he was.

So I set a goal to buy this double bunk, but to achieve it I had to be very disciplined. To me the price was astronomical and if I wanted to raise the money, I had to work hard. It wasn't easy because other kids were buying pushbikes, buying lollies and spending money. I went without because I desperately wanted to get that bunk. It took me about a year to save the deposit.

That taught me discipline in many ways. I had to do hard work. The money wasn't just going to happen. But I never wrote that goal down, where today I will write my goals and I will focus. But I must admit I didn't like sleeping with my brother at all, so every night when I went to bed I got *very* focused. It was a breakthrough. I set this goal and I achieved it.

When the double bunk arrived, one of the bedheads was the wrong bloody size. It was too small and my parents told me I was going to have to return it and get a replacement. I had waited for it for so long there was no bloody way I was going to send anything back, so Allan Friar came to the rescue when he cut the bedhead in half and stuck a piece of thin tubing inside and extended it. Allan was Betty's boyfriend and this was the first of many, many times when Allan used his handyman skills to get me out of trouble. That day marked the start of a big relationship which still continues today.

BROKEN DOORS

Material things never meant a thing to my parents. Dad would ride to work on his pushbike singing and he'd come home from work singing. He didn't see himself as poor, he saw himself as happy and successful.

For my parents' 25th wedding anniversary I bought them an off-white secondhand front door. Because the red one with all the broken panes was beyond being a door, and I was sick of it.

The red door typified what we were about as a family. We were hillbillies. And I hated it.

I hated the wind blowing through the house and it was bloody cold in that kitchen. I bought my parents a big heavy door instead. It felt like Red Gum but it was probably Cedar. It was so bloody heavy that it broke the door jamb. We fixed the jamb and that door was still in use when the house burnt down in (2005).

Even though my parents moved out of the tent, it still didn't make any bloody difference to the way they lived, the doors were never shut.

One Christmas we had a get-together with my in-laws. All the family walked in and I was last. I left the door open and someone yelled out, 'Shut the bloody door! Were you born in a tent?' And there was silence, I thought, "Mum's going to fire up" - but fortunately she didn't.

Yeah, I was brought up in a tent.

At my Mum's place the doors were always open, even in winter, so the dogs, the magpies, the bloody parrot and total strangers can come in.

MENAGERIE

We had a great childhood; it was a lot of fun. If we peed the bed, it didn't matter to my parents, there were no rules or regulations at home.

We always had heaps of pets: dogs, rabbits, ferrets, a white cocky, and a pet magpie that would pick the bloody eyes out of our shoes. At one stage we even had a pet platypus, though we didn't have it for long as the dogs got jealous and ended up killing it.

One time, Dad brought home a young injured wedge-tailed eagle. When it got bigger it started to follow Mum to town. It scared a few people and ended up raiding people's chookyards. One day it just disappeared.

Another time we tried to breed wild ducks. We raided their nests, pinched the eggs and got the chooks to hatch them, but when they got bigger the ducks went straight back to the wild.

My Mum would always called the dogs by their names, Casper, Junior, Pee Wee, Rory, Paddy ... many dogs over the years. She could always remember their names, but she never really called us kids by names; it was "you useless bastards, you buggers get inside". But that was okay - that was her.

We also had domestic ducks, pigeons, a goat, turkeys, lots of guinea pigs, baby foxes, a possum, three kangaroos and a rosella that would shit on the floor in the same place in the lounge room where it created a huge stalagmite. So we had all these bloody animals – as well as poddy calves. The only thing we never had was cats. Dad didn't like them. Mum would keep the kangaroos on the hearth in front of the fire when they were little. Chooks, ducks, any bloody animal that was orphaned or injured – would be in front of our fire. She'd even put live animals in the oven with the door open, so they'd keep warm.

The three kangaroos slept in the house in sugar bags. They would hop into their bags at night and in the morning they'd hop out. As they got bigger, they'd pinch things off the table: cups, soft drink, milk, loaves of bread, anything, especially bottles, because they were bottle fed as babies. I resented them. All the animals pissed me off. I didn't like sharing my house with them. I always believed the animals got better treatment than I did.

Nowadays I won't get too close with dogs because as a kid we always had a house full of them. And it was always the same at Mum's place, the dog always slept on her bed. Every day she bought mince steak to feed to the magpies and kookaburras, and also a packet of biscuits for the possums that lived in the wall. Who else but my Mum would have two possums living in the bloody house?

HOME LIFE

Mum and Dad had a big vegetable garden where Terry's house stands today, and they also had fruit trees and a chookyard where another house has since been built. Mum and Dad used to do a lot of gardening, it was a form of survival. Some people would swap their rabbits for our fruit, or vice versa.

We used hurricane lanterns at home until I was seven, then we got electricity. I remember the men digging the hole and erecting the power pole next to our house. My Dad never trusted electricity; he was always wary. He would get Mum to turn on the electric jug for him, he would never turn it on himself. I suppose I'm a bit like that with computers and calculators.

Clem Carr and his horse and cart did all deliveries around town, and one day he delivered our 'new' chrome and red mica (formica) table and chairs. They were wrapped up in brown paper like huge presents, and it was lots of fun undoing them.

One of the best Christmas presents I ever got was a little tin push cart. Dad painted it silver. He told me Jack Frost had painted it – Wow! Another time they brought me a plastic crane which had strings and pulleys and was featured in the front window of the toyshop. That was pretty special because my parents must have made a few sacrifices in order to buy that gift for me.

Even though it seems we didn't have much, we all got on and we were quite happy, especially when Dad got paid, because he'd often bring home a big bag of lollies for us kids. And every Saturday night he bought a two-bob block of Nestle chocolate for the bloody dogs.

NEIGHBOURS

Our first next door neighbours were the Hill family. After they moved away an Aboriginal family called the McGees moved in; there were eight of them including grandma. Mum used to say: "You couldn't get better neighbours." The father, Johnny McGee, worked at the flour mill, and Mum always said that his wife Pat was the best washer-woman she'd ever seen. She'd say: "I wish my washing was as white as Mrs McGee's." *So did I.* Washing was not one of Mum's strengths.

We got on well with the McGees. Every few weeks Dad would buy a sheep and butcher it and Mrs McGee would call out: "Are you gonna kill tonight Tooley?"

He'd say, "Yeah", in his Irish accent.

And she'd say: "Keep me the brain." We'd give her that as well as the liver and heart, because Dad wouldn't eat liver. He'd eaten too much offal when he worked on the stations.

The extended family would sometimes come to stay at McGee's, and that always meant trouble, noise and arguments. One Saturday afternoon when the footy was on, a big fight erupted and we could all hear the altercation.

Dad was working in the garden at the time. Next thing Mrs McGee came racing over to our place. She borrowed the long-handled shovel off Dad, raced back and started laying into her visitors and relations. At the same time the footy crowd who'd been walking past on the road all stopped, watched the fight and started barracking. There were so many leaning on the fence that the 20 metres of fence collapsed under their weight. Then the police came.

With all the yelling, screaming and swearing, we were sure someone must've been killed. But all Dad was worried about was getting his shovel back.

JACK D'LANTERN

The Aboriginal kids were all scared of Jack D'Lantern. I don't know where they got this spook from, but they were scared of ghosts just like us. They were an Aboriginal family – we were an Irish family - so similar in lots of ways.

We were coming back from our neighbours' place one night with the McGee kids when their Granny was coming to take them home, and she was carrying a hurricane lantern. Anyway, we spotted their Granny before they did and we stirred up the kids: "Here comes Jack D'Lantern to git you!" They were all terrified.

Granny was a shy old lady and that night she couldn't get near her grandkids. She wondered where everybody went. She didn't know that she was playing the part of the terrifying Jack D'Lantern. She didn't have a clue about what was going on. She just wandered around for ages, until she shrugged her shoulders and went home.

We lived with the fear of spooks and ghosts and the Aboriginal kids did too. At times we'd be so brave. All of us would be out and playing at night. Other times I'd be in the dark walking home alone, terrified, because I knew that he was out there. I could feel his fingers touching me as leaves brushed past my face. I could hear him running in the echoes of my footsteps. I knew his name, I knew it well: that dreaded *Boogy Man*.

We were brought up on boogy man stories, scary superstitions – like Irish stories about graveyards, bones, dead bodies. The Boogy Man – I feared him so much. It was easier to pee in the bed than to go to the outside toilet and face him.

MY PARENTS

I used to be so embarrassed about my parents. I loved my Dad but I didn't like Mum. But later in life I learned I love my Mum, warts and all. She was probably different to your Mum – so what?

I suppose my parents were different first of all because they didn't care much for material things. They'd give everything away, even our bloody bikes, toys (they were lead and they needed the money), food ... any hungry bugger could get a feed off Dad. My Dad was a generous man, he had a great belief in God.

He went to church but he never seemed to follow the Mass. I'd be watching him and he'd be having his own meditations. Dad had an incredible affinity with all living creatures. I've even seen him pet wild birds.

No other kids had the freedom we had. We'd break a window – no big deal. We were allowed to go down the river and come home when we liked. We could play outside until it was dark and we were allowed to light fires. We would sometimes walk inside the house, wringing wet from the river and dripping with mud, and Mum would say, "Get the hell outta here!" but that would be it. Nothing was ever a big deal.

BREAD

The Toc Bakery was the first bakery I ever noticed. It was a little old country bakery located 100 yards from the main centre, on the road that leads to Finley.

The shop was at the front, the house was behind the shop, and the bakehouse was at the back of the house.

Every day the bakers had to wheel the bread from the bakehouse to the front door of the shop, because they weren't allowed to go through the house.

It was a long flat low building with a side lane. There was an old warehouse up the lane near the bakery, where I would sometimes hide when wagging school. Mum used to slice the bread for the bakery and I would spot her arriving at work while I was hiding in the warehouse loft. That was my first memory of a bakery.

When Mum didn't have any money, which was quite often. She would check us all out for sixpences, but we usually didn't have any money either, so we'd have to buy stale bread. But when we got fresh bread, we couldn't help ourselves; we'd wreck the loaf by eating the guts out of it. I loved it! My first memory of bread is going to the Toc bread shop and getting it.

As a kid I always wanted to make money, and when I was 12 I bought two poddy calves, which I tried to raise on stale bread at 50c a bag. That killed one of them. It ate so much bread it burst!

WAGGING

I wagged school lots. It was easy because my younger brother James was in the same class as me and I'd always say: "You tell 'em I'm sick." He had to tell lies all the time to cover for my absences.

One time I was wagging school with a mate. We pinched a rowing boat and we were having a great time. The floods were up and we were floating around the farmland which was under water ... new territory.

We were floating near a big sandhill close to the shore and suddenly we heard voices and I recognised it was my sister Betty and my mate's sister, so we hid in the boat so they wouldn't see us.

We were right up in the bow when I heard Betty saying: "Look! Look at the boat ... sailing down the river, it must have broken away." They were watching; it had captured their attention. Next minute the current turned the boat right around 180 degrees and here I was staring straight at a surprised Betty, and boy did she go off! Both our sisters did. Wow, talk about trouble! My mate was never allowed to play with me again.

FATHER JOHN BYRNE

The Parish of Tocumwal was formed in 1918 when the convent was established. In 1927, the St Peter's Presbytery was formed. That was our parish, and Father John Byrne was its honcho, other priests used to call him 'Rocky' – I'm not sure why. He was an authority. He was a power. He was the Catholic priest in a small town. I considered him a big man, but I was little. We went to church every Sunday and I was an altar boy. I had to wear other people's altar clothes because we couldn't afford to buy our own.

Following his arrival in 1952, Father Byrne really made Tocumwal his home. Saturday night confessions were often late when Tocumwal was playing Deniliquin or Shepparton East. He is buried in Toc and is remembered for never missing a football match.

His enthusiasm for footy suggests he must have known Allan Jeans at the time Jeans was making his mark.

Terry, James and I worked at the presbytery, weeding, mowing, chopping wood and planting flowers. Set on an acre of land, it had a garage, a chook shed, a woodshed, fruit trees, lots of roses, poppies and a big lawn. The presbytery and convent are now private homes.

I started working for Father Byrne when I was nine and he paid me five bob for a Saturday morning's work, which was a lot of money at the time. You could go to the pictures and really pig out on that sort of money. Father Byrne was very authoritarian and very strict – you had to do everything 'properly'. *Hail Mary full of grace, the Lord is with you – blest are you among women – and blest is the fruit of your womb, Jesus.*

I would look at somebody in the congregation and I would crack up laughing and I couldn't stop. I'd get the bloody giggles. Even today as a public speaker, I don't look at anybody because when I was an altar boy the eye contact would make me crack up. *O Lord, hear and heed my prayer...* Years later, when I was 15, I joined the Manchester Unity of Oddfellows because my boss was in it. I cracked up three times on the night of my initiation. They had to take me outside just like Father Byrne did, because I was having a laughing fit.

I would stuff up so many times on that altar. *Hail Mary full of grace, the Lord is with you...* Laugh! Cacking in prayer, in anything. *Sing to the Lord a song not sung before...* I would say the wrong words at the wrong times. I could never remember Hail Marys. *Hail Mary, Mother of God...*

But Father Byrne would put up with me. He pulled my ear so many times because I'd forget to ring the bell. I'd ding the donger at the wrong time or I'd bring water instead of wine. I was always in trouble. And although I was a real nuissance and kill myself laughing, he would still get me up there again, even though he had plenty of other altar boys to choose from.

The fear of Hell was horrific and I suffered all that stuff, but today I'm not scared of Hell at all; I've already been there. As a kid I thought I was probably going to spend my life in purgatory, though it didn't worry me enough to change my behaviour.

Talking to my altar boy mates years later – they all told me that they got into the bloody altar wine. And that's how they coped.

I wish I'd got into the altar wine; maybe I would have coped a bloody lot better. Or maybe not!

THE DEVIL IN MY SLEEVE

Every Christmas Eve we'd all go to the pictures before attending midnight Mass. One day we went down the river to check out a fallen tree and we found it was full of bats, so we grabbed a few. They were wriggling around but we got them home. Imagine four Toole brothers hurling bats at each other in a tiny bedroom. We'd throw them, they'd half fly and then we'd grab them again. We were having such a great time that we took the bats with us to the pictures where we let them go inside the theatre. Bloody hell – chaos! The bats were flying everywhere and it was quite funny. Next thing I got hit in the back of the head with a half eaten devon sausage. I picked it up and of course threw it on. I knew where the sausage had come from – it was from my big brother Mickey. You wouldn't believe it, a theatre full of people, and I was the guy who got hit by the sausage!

After the devon sausage incident, we trundled off to church where we arrived a little bit late, so they made us go down the front, right down to the altar. There was not even an altar pew, we had to kneel on the floor. *The tabernacle, the cloth, the chalice, statues, candles, very Italian-looking...*

So there we were, kneeling. I was wearing one of those grey school coats someone had given me and it started itching. *Let the heavens rejoice...*Sitting there praying I thought: "There's something here...?" There couldn't be, maybe the shoulder pad had slipped and I kept thinking: "There's nothing ... nothing ... it's just the pad...."

Born in holy splendor, before the morning star have I begotten you.
Then I started sweating and I was in a terrible lather and felt
everyone was looking at me, and. So I looked up my sleeve and there
was the Devil looking right back at me, ***a bat!***

I got such a fright! I flicked my arm, and watched the bat catapult
into Father Byrne's vestments and plonk at his feet where it lay on its
back shamelessly squawking, *Wark! Wark!* That really stopped the
Mass. Even though it was real embarrassing, I was so relieved to have
it out of my jacket, because I'd thought I was going bloody mad. I
thought I had the Devil up my sleeve.

Then a man got up, picked up the bat and chucked it outside.
Mum got kicked out of the Mother's Club for that.

On another occasion Mum swore at a church committee
meeting. Father Byrne, who didn't approve of Mum swearing, said:
"Tooley, you'd better leave!" So she left. Next time Father Byrne saw
Mum he said: "When are you coming back to the Guild?"

She said: "I thought you'd got rid of me."

He said: "No, you'd better get back there; that other lot's useless!"

*"They let me back in because there was no other bloody bugger that
would do the work I used to do," said Mum. "Father Byrne came up and
said to me, 'Would you clean the church every Friday? I can't ask those
other 'ladies' to do it.' I said, 'Oh thanks very much!' About 12 months
later, when I had this bloody fight with the women from church, they
turned to me and said, 'You're not a lady.' I replied, 'I know I'm not,
Father Byrne has already told me that!'"*

MUM

My Mum was incredible. She went to no end of bother over certain
little things most people wouldn't notice. For example, when
Mickey worked in the flour mill, Mum would get his dinner ready,
put a hot plate over it, wrap it in a tea towel and get one of us to hop
on the bike and take it to him. If we complained too much, she'd

hop on the bike herself, peddle the mile-and-a-bit and give him his tea.

In those days, women didn't wear slacks. Despite that handicap, Mum was a very good bicycle rider. She would dink us kids for five to 10 miles to go fishing, no worries – sometimes with one kid on the handles and another on the bar. Dad would have another one of us on his bike, plus all the fishing gear.

Even though she had a husband and four sons it was Mum who mostly chopped the firewood. Mum and Dad fought like cats and dogs, yelling and screaming at times, which I suppose was pretty normal, but they did love each other.

We had a dream childhood because everything was exciting and we lived amongst nature. My parents loved fishing, they would catch Red Fin, Murray Cod, Bream and Yellowbelly. We all fished. For years I hated eating fish because I saw it as 'poor person's food'. Today, I enjoy eating fish. My parents caught a lot of their food and grew most of their own vegies because Dad was on a very low wage.

TOUGH LOVE

We listened to *Dad & Dave* and all those kinds of programs on the radio. Some nights we'd sit in the main street and watch TV through the shop windows, lots of people did. Some even brought chairs. We didn't own a TV until Terry bought a black and white one when I was 13. He bought it with the money he earned working at the Toc Cordial Factory.

In a way, my brothers and sister were supporting my parents. Every one of us contributed by buying bits and pieces of furniture. My contribution was our second lot of tables and chairs, I also purchased Mum's bed that she shared with the dog. We all bought heaps of stuff for the household; I could go on and on and on...

We didn't usually sit around the table as a family at meal times. After we'd finished eating, we'd put the plates onto the floor and the dogs would lick them clean. They were our dishwashers. I usually ate my meals on my bed, and the mice would come in at night and run all over our beds looking for crumbs. My brother would be sleeping at one end and I'd be sleeping at the other and we'd feel these creatures running over us in bed. It wasn't much bloody fun, I can tell you. Sometimes I thought it was rats and I'd be too scared to poke my head up. Other times I thought the Boogy Man was in the room.

Mum and Dad used to work in the garden until dark. We had camp fires, we played under the street lights, we had bows and arrows and an old rifle plus we didn't have to do any homework. Every weekend was an adventure.

There was lots of love – sometimes tough love – but it was good. Mum was always the one who did the discipline with an ironing cord or the broom handle. She threatened to belt us which was a big joke because most of the time we were too quick for her and she couldn't catch us.

TRAINS

From Monday to Friday Dad would ride his bike to the railway station where he worked in the days when Tocumwal was a big railway town.

There were lots of rail lines, big gantries and a huge goods shed where Dad worked as a labourer. In those days the railway station was a hive of activity, a really busy place. Every year the circus would come to town by rail and the elephants would shunt the carriages. They'd bring everything on the trains – lions, monkeys...the lot. They'd put up tents around the carriages (which were really cages) and we'd have to pay money to get a look at the animals, it was like going to the zoo and very exciting.

Peter Sadler was one of my mates. His Dad worked on the railways too. At one stage we'd wagged primary school all week and by Friday we were getting bored. There was only one thing left for us to do: run away from home (we'd done everything else). Peter and I decided that we should go to Melbourne, get a job and earn some money. I had 15 bob hidden in my bedroom and I also had a map of Victoria to figure out where Melbourne was. So I went home, got the map, grabbed the coins, met Peter near the Red Bridge and waited for a train to slow down so that we could jump on.

After watching two trains travelling too fast for our little legs, we were a bit scared and soon worked out that we could only board a stationary train, so we walked through the cattle yards - until we reached the far end of the big railway station. There we undid the ropes and got under tarps and into a steel carriage. So as not to be spotted, we had to be quick because people were working everywhere. I scrambled inside but when I got in, my money fell straight out of my pocket and we couldn't get it back because our little arms couldn't reach down between the big bags of produce.

While we were under the tarps, we thought: "I hope they don't come along and tie them ropes up, because otherwise we'll be in real trouble, we'll be stuck." But they didn't.

Then the train started to move and through a little hole, Peter saw his father checking every carriage and writing their numbers down. I too saw my father working on the station as we were leaving it. When we crossed the Red Bridge and got into the bush, we flicked back the canvas cover and poked our heads out. The wind was in our hair and everything was great. Freedom, at last!

Eventually we arrived at Shepparton – and neither of us had ever been there before. The train started to shunt back-forwards, back-forwards before grinding to a slow halt. When it stopped we hopped out and went downtown.

Shepparton was a big place and we didn't know where to go. We ended up trying to sleep in a disused toilet, but it was too cold. Peter started missing his parents and getting upset. I was acting tough and wasn't showing it. So we went back to the railways and hopped back into the carriage where it was warmer than being in the toilets.

When daylight came we had to find our way out of Shepparton – because by this time we had agreed that we were going back home - whichever way that was. At last someone pointed us in the right direction and we hitch-hiked. The trip took quite a few rides but we both reached home that afternoon. I met Mum walking along the road, she was reading the newspaper. When she saw me snapped: "Where have you been? Your father's bin looking for you!"

Then I found Dad, who was so grateful to see me. I moved away so that he couldn't see me cry, but when she lost sight of me, Mum started crowing: "See, he's pissed off again! He's gone! He's gone! You should have given him a belting!" But I hadn't gone anywhere. I only stepped outside so he couldn't see my tears. I realised how much I had hurt Dad by running away.

It was a big deal; they even had the police looking for us.

BLESS THIS HOUSE

My Dad prayed all the time. He even had an altar in the bedroom. Every morning before he went to work he would bless the garden and bless the whole place. The Irish do that. They bless themselves every time they go past cemeteries. They bless themselves when they approach danger. They bless themselves many times every day.

If you dropped a knife, someone else had to pick it up for you. It was really bad luck if you did it yourself. And if Dad was fishing and you said to him, "You won't going to catch any fish here", he'd pack up and leave – because he reckoned you'd put the moz on him. He was a very superstitious bugger.

I pray today because I believe in the power of prayer. I don't go to church. I was brought up on the Catechism, but now I can't recite a Hail Mary. I can't even recite the Lord's Prayer.

But I strongly believe there is a higher power; a God of my own understanding.

There's got to be something greater than Tom O'Toole; I sure know that!

BREADWINNER

CHAPTER THREE

BREAD OF LIFE

> *To identify schools with*
> *education is to confuse*
> *salvation with the church.*
> **Ivan Illich, Deschooling Society**

Despite everything I've written, my father would never have considered himself a financial failure. He had more riches than I'll ever have. Although I couldn't see it at the time, because I hated living in bloody poverty, he had success, and I can confidently say that because today I know that riches come from within.

We are all born rich. From my father I learned about self-worth, peace and empathy with nature.

FINDING MONEY, SELLING BOTTLES

As a kid I was very interested in money, yet my father wasn't. I wanted boats, I wanted push bikes, I wanted material things. And, to achieve it, I was prepared to work at anything. *Anything for money – anything.* While every other kid would be out playing sport and doing normal things, there I would be, trying to earn money catching river crays, even in the freezing cold.

I'd put earning money before anything else. I was never interested in Rock and Roll, the Rolling Stones, the Beatles and all that. I was never interested in school or sport, I was too busy working. Work, work, work and more work. Everyone else was out partying, but I was too busy trying to make money.

So I was very entrepreneurial at an early age - there's not too many kids who pay off their own bed at the age of 11, but I did. *Anything for money - anything.* On the way to school I'd sometimes nick grub-infested apples from a little orchard. They were shocking apples but I still managed to get a few bob for them. Then I got another brilliant idea. I thought: "I'm going to try gambling."

I'd work all day Saturday and then I'd lose my whole 10 bob on cards! So I stopped bloody gambling as soon as I figured there was no fast money to be made because it held no other appeal for me. My Dad had a completely different attitude. He used it for recreation and he got lots of enjoyment out of betting. He would listen to the bloody races on the radio all day long and bet every Saturday. A real small better, my Dad was. He would only place two bob bets.

I had no interest in sport, except of course if there was money to be made, which there was if you kept a sharp eye on the spectators near the bar at the Toc Footy Oval every second Saturday during a football match. At the ground there were three makeshift bars – tents - where they sold beer and other drinks. I'd hang around the counter watching to see if anybody dropped money. If they did, it would sink with a little puff into the sawdust floor. I'd remember where those coins fell and when the match was over and the people had gone home, I'd come back around sunset and pick up the coins. That way, I made good money every second Saturday in winter.

Another way of making money was to look for soft drink bottles by the side of the road, because in those days people chucked them straight out of car windows, along with everything else. I'd walk along the side of those roads searching for bottles because the returns had a value of threepence or sixpence.

FIRST JOB, FIRST BUSINESS

When I was in primary school Father Byrne gave me my first regular paying job and I kept working for him until I was 13. I had to turn up on time though. And I had to do it properly or I'd be in trouble. He was a very 'straight' man and a good priest. He was good for me. He didn't mollycoddle us; he treated us tough and rough – but he also took care of us. For example, when necessary, he even took us to the dentist in his car.

(I bought my first set of dentures when I was 14. That was my second big goal and I paid for them myself. It took me one whole year to save the $80, most of which I earned catching and selling crayfish illegally. Dad always said, "Get 'em out son, it's the best thing you can do," so I got my top teeth pulled out. Dad sometimes got it wrong. I would love to have my real teeth today. Dad also encouraged me to smoke. Funnily enough, none of us boys took it up.)

However, selling crays was only one of my money-earning ventures. Other jobs included working in the flour mill where I'd stand taking string out of the wheat bags for eight hours a day.

I also worked on farms, where I'd walk over acres and acres looking for burrs, which I would cut it out with a hoe. It was a hard job. The hoe blistered my hands and there was lots of walking.

Another terrible job was hay carting. I'd get sunburned and I would buckle at the knees, lifting those heavy bales. And the hay was itchy and scratchy when it got on my arms and into my clothes.

I also mowed lawns, did gardening and all sorts of jobs. *Anything for money – anything.*

And I used to catch rabbits and fish, which I would sell to the neighbours. My Dad also caught rabbits and fish, but most of the time he just gave them away. And that was the difference between Dad and me, and why I reckon he was born rich. He'd give the things away that I would sell.

Technically, dealing in gemstones was my first business. I went into gems in quite a big way. While I was still at school I bought a shed on hire purchase and paid it off in instalments. My parents disliked hire purchase. They only ever used it once, but I had complete confidence that I could meet the repayments. So having got myself a shed, what I needed next was a cement floor. I had no money to spare, so I pinched the gravel off the council piles at the side of the road. I had to barrow it over a long distance. It was pretty bloody heavy and I thought my arms were going to be pulled out their sockets.

Having got a shed and a cement floor, I set up a tumbler. Next, I acquired a few tools, including a little diamond saw, so I was able to clean and polish stones myself. When I'd completed a load, I'd hitch-hike the 50 miles to Shepparton where I would sell them and buy more uncut stones and more grit. Then I'd go home, polish and cut them, and come back again.

```
Dad was quite proud of my cottage industry
           and he would bring people
            to the shed to show me off.
        But I'd know they were out there,
        so I'd hide and stay real quiet.
       They'd think, 'Where did Tom go?'
          They didn't know I was hiding
              in Tom Toole's shed.
```

I was a bit different from the rest of the family, because I had this thing about money. I knew it was my only way out. But my brothers and my sister put other things before money and were not entrepreneurial, though of course, all the boys had odd jobs and they all worked for Father Byrne. They fished a bit, caught crays, and two of my brothers were into shooting - but I've never been into shooting anything except my brothers. One of them, who never owned a home or a car for years, called me a 'capitalist pig'. *Okay, where's the gun?*

HIGH SCHOOL

When I got too big for the primary school desks they sent me to the Catholic high school in Finley which was 35 km away. It closed after my first year. Then I went to the state high school, also in that town. Finley was twice as big as Toc. The town itself was almost named Ulupna back in the 1870s, but in the end it was named after F C Finley, a surveyor who had the job of sorting out the squatters' land rights.

High school was so hard for me because I hadn't learned the basics. I learned nothing in primary school, and I mean *nothing*. I didn't even know where Australia was on the map. And because I didn't even know my two-times tables, I was the only kid in maths class who was allowed to read comics instead of doing work. While everyone else was doing arithmetic, all I had to do was (1) read Donald Duck and war comics, and (2) remember not race across the desks and out the window. I didn't have to worry about anything else. Everybody else had to do work, but I had no understanding of maths. I used to rule up my page -- and that's about all I did in class, nothing else.

I teamed up with a couple of other misfits at school. I was a loner and a misfit.

I was half-Irish and I always felt I was different. I was called a 'Mick' and we copped all the Catholic-Irish jokes. We were also the 'half-Irish and half-mad Bungaree Savages' (Bungaree is a little place in Victoria where they grow lots of potatoes). Yes, they called me the mad bad-tempered Irish kid and I proved them right every time.

I was never into sport (plus we couldn't afford the uniforms) so on sports days I'd have to stand outside the headmaster's office. Sometimes he'd punish me by making me take off my shoes and run around the oval, through the bindies and mud. But I still wouldn't play sport.

Other times he'd take me into the staff car park, hand me a bucket and tell me to pick through the gravel and fill it with white stones. When I'd finish, I'd take the full bucket to him and he would scatter the white stones back onto the driveway. Then he'd make me pick them all up again. I did that many times. And I got to resent my state school teachers because they didn't care for me and they were tough. Whereas Father Byrne was also tough, but he cared a lot.

Father Byrne died when I was in my first year of high school and that was really sad. Father Byrne was a role model. He had a real certainty about life, and about right and wrong. I don't know whether I've got that clarity of life today; but he had it, as did my Dad.

I left school at 14. I didn't even finish second year – what was the sense?

GRRR!

Because there were more kids in attendance, the state school was a much tougher place than the Catholic school. For example, in my first year at the Catholic high school, they initiated the new kids by sticking their heads in the baptismal font. When it was my turn, they went to grab me and they all just stopped. They wouldn't touch me. I had an 'aura' and I was very lucky that way. But the State school was a much bigger water hole, and I had a few scary moments with the bigger kids.

I wasn't a good fighter but I had an incredible temper. I remember one guy walked up and said to me, 'I reckon I can belt you' and I was shittin' myself.

Although I couldn't really defend myself, I got a wild look in my eye and said: 'Do ya reckon? *Grrr!*' and then he never tried me. I had an Irish temper and I wouldn't back down. I would go anyone -

even a teacher. I would pick things up and wave them in people's faces. I was a dangerous boy. I carried a pocket knife and I wasn't scared to pull it either.

One time I upset our Aboriginal neighbours when I stabbed their son. He always wanted to fight me and I didn't like that, the bastard. He was a good fighter too; one day he hassled me so I stabbed him. His parents were quite upset, so I hid under the bed until it was all sorted out. I didn't do a lot of damage, but getting stabbed is still not nice.

Another time we were playing cops and robbers and Terry shot me in the middle of the forehead with an air rifle.

I started yelling: "I'm going to tell Mum! I'm going to tell Mum!" and I went racing home with blood squirting out of my head.

As I ran off to the house, Terry begged: "Don't tell Mum!"

I ran inside and, of course, Mum asked me: "What happened?"

I said: "I ran into a stick."

Then Terry ran in after me and yelled, "I didn't mean it! I didn't mean to shoot him!" and dobbed himself right in.

For years after I believed I was mad because I reckoned that bullet was still in my head.

I knew I was mad at school.

I kept asking myself, why am I mad?

JOBS

After leaving school my first job was washing bottles and stacking drinks at the Tocumwal Cordial Factory. I knew the place pretty well because I had worked there on and off during the school holidays since I was 12.

That was my first proper job, and Terry used to dink me to work on his Honda 50 scooter, even though he wasn't supposed to because he was only a L-plate driver. In my time about six people worked there and the business never grew to anything because the big soft drink companies muscled in and dominated the market. Terry worked there all his life, retiring at the end of 1999.

The owner was a coin collector, so one of my jobs was to sort his coins. Sometimes I spent all day sorting them. He'd buy a 44 gallon drum full of pennies and I'd have to sort them all into categories - 1948 pennies, 1964, 1938, 1958, 1917 ... and so on. It was just like picking up white stones really.

And that was my first job, being a little 14-year old shit-kicker around the Toc Cordial Factory, sorting coins, cleaning bottles, weeding the garden and filling in time. I also kept up all my other jobs too - earning extra money by cutting gemstones and crayfishing with illegal drum nets. I just kept on working. However, I really missed Father Byrne's iron hand to guide me.

I saw Melbourne for the first time when I was 15. Until then Shepparton, with its population of 30,000, was my idea of a big city. *I thought the Red Bridge in Toc was bloody huge, but you should see them bridges there!* I thought Shepparton had big shops until I saw what they had in Melbourne! I stared into those windows and I wanted to buy everything. There was so much of everything. I still love looking at shops today. Furthermore, there was no end to the city – Carlton, St Kilda, Elsternwick, Warrandyte, Dandenong, Sunshine…the houses just went on and on. So that was Melbourne, I thought: *Bloody hell.* I didn't know what to make of it except to realise there was a much bigger world out there, and I was curious about where else that Red Bridge would lead.

SECOND NEW THING

Meanwhile, conditions were improving at home. Mum and Dad had decided to actually buy something brand new. Hoorah! They never bought new clothes, never bought new tools, never bought new doors, never used new timber, never, never new.

The exception was once when I was little and Mum and Dad bought red mica and chrome table and chairs. I don't know how come they had money to buy them but they were *new*.

Twenty years later I bought new tables and chairs as a present for my parents.

They were timber veneer and chrome, with seats upholstered in green and white vinyl, but during the first week the cocky chewed holes in the vinyl – well, I was going to pull his bloody head off, I was!

The second new thing was a fridge, bought when I was 15. Mickey bought the first fridge, the creamy coloured one, but Dad bought the white Kelvinator, *wow!* Not only that, but he bought it on hire purchase, which he never liked. It was his only hire purchase.

While the fridge was still 'new' I lost my temper with Dad and I threw a knife at him. He ducked and it hit the fridge. Dad was so upset! I might have killed the bugger but he wasn't worried about that; he was only worried about the mark on the fridge.

It wasn't a frost-free model, and we were supposed to regularly defrost it. One day Mum got impatient and while she was defrosting it she stuck a knife in and ended up poking the gasline. We couldn't mend it and next time we defrosted it, the gas kept leaking. Then Mum and Dad figured that if they never defrosted the fridge they'd never have to get it re-gassed. So forever after the fridge never got defrosted. When the ice built up they just smashed it with a hammer. Well, they didn't always remember and the ice built up so much that it broke the inside freezer door and you couldn't use the freezer, which became just a solid block of ice. In time the bottom rusted out, but they still kept using it for the next 35 years. It was real value for money.

BAKING IN TOCUMWAL

Here I was at 16 trying to figure out what to do with my life. Dad always encouraged me immensely in whatever I was dreaming about at the time – going into trucks, renting boats, etc. But Mum always told me I was a useless little bugger and things like that.

"I never gave a bugger what Tom did," said Mum. "Tom said, 'I don't know what I want to be – I just want to be an apprentice.' He called at the butcher's, who didn't need an apprentice. So he went up to Hammer's Bakery and Frank Hammer said, 'Start in the morning'. The baker's shop was where a motel now stands, behind Tattersall's Pub. That's where Tom learned how to bake bread. And where I bloody learned how to slice.

"Tom took after his father because Chris always worked. Tom was a hard worker, not really for himself, but for the family.

"I'm proud of Tom."

The butcher didn't want me, so I applied at the bakery and Frank Hammer put me on straight away. I started the next day, working a six day week.

This was the same bakery near our hideout when wagging school, and where Mum had a part-time job slicing bread – Hammer's of Tocumwal.

Although I didn't know it at the time, in 1967 when I started my apprenticeship, the politics of baking were really beginning to take shape. In Victoria, Metro Bakers, who had large plants, started running bread into country areas. Sunicrust Bread from Ballarat ran bread into the Horsham area of north west Victoria. Plus the Army contract for bread at Puckapunyal was delivered out of Melbourne. Then the local people of Seymour started to buy bread from the Army base. The independent bakeries were on the way out.

To protect themselves from this, the Bakers of Victoria established a clause passed through Parliament in 1967 that bread could only be delivered up to 50 km from where it was baked. So large bakeries bought out the local bakeries and simply used their premises as depots.

Millers especially, tried to secure their trade by buying out bakeries or taking over their assets to secure debts. For example, Wise Brothers was establishing a range of country bakeries, and all this was going on in the background while I was doing my apprenticeship, and I didn't know a thing about it.

One morning I came to work and saw that Frank was fast asleep on the bench. That wasn't so surprising because if the yeast was a bit slow we would often sleep on the bench while waiting for the doughs. But on that particular morning Frank was lying down because he had stuck his hand in a machine, so all of a sudden I had take over everything. It was a new experience and I think I did well. Here I was at 16, running the place until he got in a relief baker, then he sold out to Baker Boy, who closed down Hammer's Bakery of Tocumwal. Another local business shut, so I continued my apprenticeship in Shepparton.

LEAVING HOME

Baker Boy, later Home Pride, was a big company and it bought the Tocumwal Bakery and agreed to take over my apprenticeship, so I had to leave home to work in Shepparton which had a really big bakery. So at 16 I was in the big wide world and 'on my way'. Although I did miss Toc and those Murray River days, I didn't miss my family much.

At this stage of my life I knew there was something different about me. I somehow *knew* I was going to be a success in business even though I had no money. I was under-aged to get into pubs, I was bloody hopeless with women and I suffered heaps of fears, but I still knew I was going to make it somehow. I don't know where I got that 'knowing' from, but I've always had it.

The people at Baker Boy weren't real nice. They played awful tricks on me. A few of them even tried to belt me up. They treated me like a total dickhead.

Well, I was a Toole.

MY FIRST CAR

Under Victorian state law I wasn't allowed to have a driving licence until I was 18, so I got my car licence at Tocumwal in New South Wales where the legal age was 17. I was living in Shepparton Victoria at the time, and luckily the Toc policeman knew me because when I worked there he used to come into the bakehouse every morning to pick up his free loaf. When I went for my licence I ballsed up real bad and he gave me a hard time. He finally, went easy on me and I got it.

Now that I had a licence, I needed a car because I'd moved from Shepparton to Beechworth, so I bought a Simca with a hole where the bloody starter motor should have been. I was in a hurry to get going, so I bought it even though the owner didn't want to sell it to me until he'd fixed it. The guy said: "Driving without a starter motor is okay – except for one thing: if you stop Tom, you're buggered." It was a scary drive but I made it back okay.

A few days later I decided to drive the Simca to Albury to pick up a starter motor from the wreckers'. Like I said, Albury is the big smoke. They have things like traffic lights, which I'd never had to deal with before. Yes, I stalled the bloody car in the main street, Dean Street, and I had to be push-started right in the centre of town. To a Tocumwal kid who'd only just got his driving licence, stalling in the main street of a big town is a pretty scary experience. The traffic lights were confusing enough without having to worry about stalling.

Later on I bought a Volkswagen on hire purchase. I bought and insured it, in my Dad's name but I ended up pranging it. (My Dad had a licence but couldn't drive, because his legs were buggered, a legacy of fighting in Ireland.)

Here I was, 18 years old and I'd never spoken to Mum or Dad over the phone before – how could I? – they didn't have one. Anyway I pranged my car and I needed to explain it all to Dad. I wasn't sure whether or not he realised that I'd forged his name.

So I rang the railway station and a guy with a thick Irish accent answered the phone.

I couldn't figure out who it was so I said, "Can I talk to Chris Toole?" and the voice said: "This is him speaking."

So I tried again, and this time the voice replied: "This *is* Chris Toole."

The Irishman with this incredible accent was my father! People always used to say, 'Geez, your Dad's got a thick accent' but I never realised it until that day when I didn't recognise his voice, because I'd never heard him speak on a phone!

Anyway, I told Dad what I'd done and he said: "Tom, do whatever you've got to do." So I rang up the insurance company and told them I was Chris Toole, and everything worked out in the end.

BAKING IN BEECHWORTH

From Shepparton, my new bosses sent me to work at the Home Pride Bakery in Camp Street, Beechworth, (now the site of the Fiddleback Bar & Restaurant and the Carriage Motor Inn). Because of the 50 km 'runs', this bakery was really a wholesaler, though they also ran a little shop.

(In those days, the Beechworth Bakery was known as The Ideal Café & Milk Bar with a drapery next door. I went there a couple of times, and I remember liking the building, never imagining it would one day be mine.)

I enjoyed living in Beechworth; it was a run down sort of a town, nothing like it is today. There were a lot of empty shops and a few were boarded up and being lived in. Somebody lived in what is now the ice cream shop, someone else lived in the Provender…I could go on and on. In those days there was quite a bit of stigma attached to Beechworth because of the asylum and the jail. And it was quite possible to run into someone who was totally off their rocker. But that was okay.

I lived on the bakery premises, paying $12 per week full board out of my $15 wages. I owned a car, but I couldn't drive it for the next five months because I couldn't afford the petrol. I had very little money for extra food, which is tough when you're young and hungry.

The family I was living with had three little kids who ate small servings. But I was a growing boy and I wanted to eat like a horse. I'd want to bloody *eat*, and so I'd get into the bakery bins looking for mouldy pies. The mould was only on the top, so I'd pull the tops off and eat them.

I've always loved bakery food.

They made me production manager at 17 because Murray, our regular manager, broke a bone in his neck and was off work for three months.

All up, I ended up spending 11 months in Beechworth. When the time came for me to attend bakery school in Melbourne, I quit that job because I was too frightened to go; I knew I'd fail. I had no hope. I never did well at school and I couldn't see that changing, whether it was primary, high or bakery school. I went back to work in New South Wales and I changed over my apprenticeship papers. All up, I changed my apprenticeship papers three times in order to dodge school.

NO SOAPBOX

When I was young I never had girlfriends. I had very low self-worth. I was fascinated by girls; they took up a lot of my headspace. I always wanted them, but I was frightened to make a move because I felt I was ugly. As a young fella I was obsessed with sex and all the normal stuff.

I fell in love with lots of girls, but they didn't know about it.

I had a couple of girlfriends when I was 17 and 18, but nothing worth reporting.

I probably would have met more girls if I'd gone to pubs, but I was never into drinking or anything like that. I didn't have the time – work was my escapism. I didn't get into sport. And I've never got into politics or rock 'n roll, although I always read the newspapers. I had my agenda, which was to get on with life and not worry too much about the things that didn't affect me.

Even today I don't worry about GST, taxes or anything like that. It's all going to work out one way or the other. Worrying about it isn't going to help, it's only going to waste my time.

You won't hear me getting on my soapbox about whoever is in government. Politics was never big in my family, I can't even remember it being mentioned. Nowadays, I can meet politicians from either side. I've got nothing against them. I wouldn't have their job for all the money in the world.

MY FIRST BLOCK OF LAND

While I was doing my apprenticeship, I wanted to buy a block of land but I couldn't get the money from any bank. So I rang Dad and told him my problem. He said: "Come on down, I'll take a few hours off work and we'll go to the bank together."

For Dad to take time off work was really something.

So we went to the Tocumwal National Bank. We walked in and sat in this wood-grain panelled office while I watched the bank manager belittle my father, who was still paying off our family home, which cost only 200 pounds. I felt he'd humiliated my Dad, and after all that I still didn't get the bloody money.

That episode made me so much more determined. Instead of buying just one block of land, I bought two, and I got the loan through ESANDA.

Throughout my early business years I got all my money through finance companies or through vendor finance because banks never liked me. Even when I was in business, I couldn't borrow from banks for a long long time. I resented the banks for that.

I also felt for my father because he was a proud man. Later in life, when I sent him a cheque for something or other, he seemed to compensate for that awful moment in the bank manager's by emphasising that he had a lot of credibility with banks.

"Dear Tom, I received that cheque," he wrote in May 1983. "There was no need - if we get into trouble I have only to ask at the bank; my name is very good there. But thanks a million."

WISING UP

When Home Pride Bakery increased my pay to $18 per week and promoted me to production manager, I was a little bit in demand and a couple of other bakeries offered me jobs. I was offered a job at Cavanagh's at Cobram which I turned down because I had already accepted a job at Wise Brothers at Albury. In a way, it was a big deal.

Wise Brothers owned the Tocumwal Flour Mill that I'd worked in earlier. Somehow through all this wheeling and dealing they had built up what seemed to me like quite an empire.

So I went to Albury and worked for Wise. They sent me on the delivery run to Culcairn and gave me a six-cylinder car – wow! I had never driven anything so powerful. I did big drifts around the farm roads and drove like a madman along those flat country stretches. Instead of Mad Dog Morgan terrorising the country with a six-gun, it was Mad Tom with a steering wheel and six cylinders.

In those days I lived in Lavington, a suburb of Albury, and I started to visit the pubs, especially the Astor, and I did a lot of wild things with my friends when I was 18-19 years old. I wasn't much of a drinker, so crazy things happened on the odd occasion when I got into it. I remember one night I had a few rums and I was as full as a fat lady's sock. I started working in the bakehouse at midnight and the fumes and the smell of the yeast got to me and, aaagh, I had to do the big spit. I ran out the door of the bakehouse and threw up. I lost my dentures in the bloody gutter and I thought, "I'm never going to drink rum again." So I didn't drink for ages.

And then I did.

I had good times as an apprentice. I even met Mr Geoff Wise and I had to wash his Mercedes a few times. I looked up to him, but I wouldn't go as far as to call him a role model. The person I really admired was my immediate boss, Frank Sinnett. He lived just up the road from where I was boarding and he influenced me a lot.

FRANK & FAIR

Frank was a hard boss but he was very fair. I remember talking to him in his office many times, as he sat behind his big desk while giving me advice. Frank looked after me; he knew I was keen to get ahead. I always felt he was 'watching out' for me, and I promised myself that someday I'd get a desk just like his.

Frank got me doing heaps and heaps of overtime, and he also had me doing some senior jobs on apprenticeship wages. I must admit that pissed me right off, but today I realise that the knowledge and experience I received was far more valuable than the dollars I'd missed out on.

Frank knew more about me than he let on. For example, even as an apprentice I used to earn extra money on Friday and Saturday nights by rabbiting around the hills of Albury. Having caught them, I'd go back to the bakery where I cleaned them. I was good at 'getting into' places. It's a talent that I had.

One night I was cleaning the rabbits in the sink, and next minute SHIT! The security guard did his run at a different time and he caught me. I wasn't supposed to be there and I thought I'd be in deep trouble. I was sweating on it, but I never heard anything about it from Frank, even though he must have known exactly what was going on.

I was getting my bakery ticket through a correspondence course, which Frank's daughters used to handle for me. I had no bloody idea how to do the written work. When it came time to get my ticket, the teacher came down from Sydney to conduct my baking exam.

I was shitting myself.

Frank softened the inspector up so that the questions were nice and easy, otherwise I would never have got my ticket. He and his family looked after me all right. *Thanks again Frank.*

All in all, it was a good experience. Wise Brothers had a lot of bakeries and I was lucky enough to experience working in different ones in different towns: Albury, Wagga, Culcairn, Cobram, Shepparton and Wangaratta.

'I WANT TO GO INTO BUSINESS, FRANK'

Just before completing my apprenticeship, I turned to Frank for advice and said: "I want to go into business, Frank."

"There's a business for sale at Tallangatta - go out and take a look," he replied. Well, I did take a look and I got so excited! I came back and told him all about it, and he said: "How are you going to buy it?"

"I don't know Frank, how am I going to buy it?"

He replied: "Tom, do you have any rich relations?"

"No."

"Do you buy lottery tickets?"

"No."

"How are you going to make the money?"

I said: "I don't know."

He said: "Tom, I'll tell you how you're going to make the money – *hard work*. That's the only way you're going to make money."

Well, I was devastated! There had to be a softer, easier way. I'd been working since I was 10, but I still didn't even have $20 in the bank.

I didn't really drink or smoke, I didn't party. I worked every hour I could, and here I was at 19 years of age and I still didn't have anything. I was paying off two blocks of land in Albury, I owned a bomb car and I couldn't even afford petrol or repair bills.

But nevertheless I learned an important lesson, and it was Frank who gave it to me: the knowledge that 'you have to have money to buy a business'. And I figured the fastest way to do that was to apply for a good-paying job.

A lot of my mates didn't have any dreams or goals, whereas *I did* and that made me very different from most of them. Sure, I wanted the fast cars, like they did – but I also had this over-riding goal that I wanted to get somewhere in life. I wanted to get into business, but I didn't know what sort. At first, I wanted to get into jewellery; later on I was going to be a butcher (I'm glad I didn't). And even when I got into baking I didn't know whether or not it was what I wanted to do.

But at 19 I was very focused on making money, and I found making money was very hard. Today I know that I can work as hard as possible, but if I'm not working smarter, I'm just marking time.

I didn't know that at 19. I thought I had to keep working harder

and harder

and harder

and harder and harder and harder.

One thing I knew for sure was that I didn't want to end up at 65 like my Dad who had worked hard all his life but he still never had any money. I wanted to have a home, a business and a decent car that I could hop in, turn the key and away it would go.

Even today when I am driving along in my car I am still grateful that the car isn't going to conk out, because I always had bombs when I was young. And I hated that.

In addition to our family cars I own an A-model Ford, a 1954 Jag that's being restored, a 1936 Chevrolet, a 1930 Chevrolet baker's van and a 1930 Chevrolet Bakery truck.

MANINGRIDA CALLING

One of the guys I was working with in Albury was a Jehovah's Witness. He went up to Maningrida in Arnhem Land to set up a bakery for an Aboriginal co-op.

His main objective was to teach them about Jehovah and he was giving away the job because they were tribal Aborigines – and they didn't have a bloody clue what he was on about. So the job was advertised Australia-wide and I wanted to apply for it.

I didn't know much about job applications, but I knew what an application letter looked like because Frank had just advertised for a manager and there were application letters all over his desk.

Because I was a dough-maker, I was often at the bakery by myself at night and I knew how to get into the main office. So I checked out the way the job applications were worded. Then Frank got sick and went to hospital.

I went to see him and said: "Frank, I want you do something for me."

He said: "Sorry Tom, I'm too sick."

I said: "If I write a letter, would you sign it for me?" He said yes.

So I copied all the 'good bits' off the applications I had seen on his desk, I got somebody in the office to type it up, Frank signed it, and that's how I applied for the bakery manager's job at Maningrida in the Northern Territory.

DOOINIT

Over those early years I learned that if you first set your goals, then save hard, your dreams will begin to come true. I learned that good things happen if you force yourself to take the initiative and just *do things*. You might start by buying a chrome double bunk and end up with two blocks of land.

My advice to any young 'Tom Toole' reading this book is: have some dreams, set some goals and especially – *especially* - don't listen to them bloody dream-takers.

I always ask kids, where do you want to be in five years?

No one ever asked me that question.

It took until I was 32 before a counsellor said to me: "Tom, where do you want to be in five years?"

And I didn't know the answer; I was too busy doing it, *dooinit, dooinit!*

Where do YOU want to be?

To me, that is a pretty profound question. Today I write out my life goals and my business goals. But at 19, yes I had goals, but I didn't have them written. I didn't start writing my goals on paper until I reached my mid-30s and, boy, did that dramatically change my life!

"Write your goals down and date them" is the best advice I can give. If they're not on paper, they're not on this planet as far as I'm concerned.

And don't leave school without an education. I did, because I lost the plot. I always thought it was up to the teachers or somebody else. I always felt limited because of poverty and my lack of education. But, fortunately, I also recognised that money could give me the freedom I wanted, and I was right in a sort of way. But it took more than money to straighten out Tom Toole. Today I realise that if you think that money is going to solve all your problems – you've got problems.

DICKHEAD & SHOVEL

Today I'm in love with life and rarin' to go. Every morning I wake up, very grateful I'm alive. The secret is to have an attitude of gratitude. If I am grateful, I have energy and I'm motivated. If I'm ungrateful, I have no energy and I'm demotivated and shitty.

Back then, I had an incredible inferiority complex. I felt so inadequate. I even felt awkward using a telephone because numbers are not one of my strengths. I hadn't long mastered the circular dial and the buggers brought in the push-button type!

I had such a fear of authority, (I realise today that I picked that up from my father). I couldn't even really sign my name in public. If somebody was watching me, I would have a hard time signing.

I was always made fun of and I felt that was partly because of my name. I always used to get called 'Dickhead' and 'Shovel' and 'Tool'. Today I don't use nicknames for anyone. I was a very angry young man. I resented people who had an education and I resented people with money – *yet that's what I wanted most, money and education!*

I have an education today because I read a lot and I travel a lot – but don't ask me to remember the names of all the places I've travelled to, let alone spell them!

For me to look up a dictionary or look up a phone book is a massive job. Because I still can't spell properly. I'll be looking under 'C' instead 'K' - so I'm hopeless like that.

I was always told I was hopeless, and now here I am saying I am hopeless.

BREADWINNER

CHAPTER FOUR

BOMA BOMA

*The Aborigines do not think
differently from us; they
merely observe material data
in a more mystical way.*
**James G Cowan,
The Elements of the
Aborigine Tradition**

L es Holt, the guy who started the Maningrida Bakery, was the Jehovah's Witness who moved back to Albury and left the position of bakery manager, so I applied and got his job. It took a lot of courage for me to apply; not only was it a management position – but I'd never heard of Maningrida! I've never been big on geography.

Anyway, I found where Maningrida was, and I flew up there ready to start work. It was my first time on a big plane.

Maningrida is in Arnhem Land on the north coast of Australia, 370 km east of Darwin. I was there in 1972-73 when almost all Aborigines lived on missions, cattle stations or government settlements like Maningrida, an Aboriginal-controlled reserve that can't be entered by whitefellas without a permit.

With an Aboriginal population of 1100-1200 and a white population of 150 when I went there, Maningrida was the sixth biggest town in the Northern Territory. The Aborigines I employed didn't necessarily all speak the same language, which made it pointless for me to learn their lingo. I was told there were 11 different tribes and 23 dialects there.

I was employed by the Maningrida Progress Association (MPA) and Glen Bagshaw was the big boss. The MPA was in charge of the supermarket, the fishing enterprise, a building company, the bakery, the Hasty Tasty, plus the market gardens which was run by Bob Collins. Bob later became a Federal Labor politician, then later in life really hit the news scandalously.

There wasn't much to do in Maningrida, unless you fancied swimming with the crocs. There was no TV and you couldn't pick up radio stations, except for bloody Radio China which broadcast Communist propaganda. Some people played cassettes, but I wasn't into any music.

There had been an attempted plane high-jack shortly before my arrival, so when I got off at the Darwin Airport the place was full of security guards armed with machineguns. The military presence was my first culture shock; the climate was the second. When I got off the plane, I thought I was standing in the blast of the engines, but it wasn't the engines – it was the heat. I couldn't believe it. I was wearing shorts and long white socks at the time, and wow – did my legs get sunburned! Later I walked over to Fanny Bay Beach and got even more burned.

By the end of the day I looked like an uncooked chook.

BIG MONEY

I stayed one night in Darwin before flying to Maningrida. While sitting in the plane, a DC3, someone asked me why I was going there? I replied that I had to teach the Aborigines to bake bread. This person said: "Tom you can't teach them buggers, they're *tribal!* And if you do teach them, you're gonna be out of a job." Well, there wasn't much truth in that.

The Aborigines couldn't understand how come there were '20 ounces to a pint' and '16 ounces' to a pound – neither could I, so we got along famously. So what if they couldn't read or write? I wasn't much good at those things either. So what if they didn't wear shoes? I didn't wear shoes. And today my Mum still doesn't wear shoes much. So we had a fair bit in common, which is why I actually *could* teach them.

Professionally speaking, I had completed my apprenticeship before leaving New South Wales and I attained my Craftsman's Certificate on 30 April, 1972, within three months of arriving in the Territory. It was my first job with full qualifications and on a full wage. I got big money too – $6000 a year. I was a 'man' at last.

Sure, I knew how to bake bread, make a bit of pastry and some cakes but I wasn't a great baker, (I'm no great baker, even today). I mightn't have been a great baker, but at least I'd have a go – boots n all. And even though I was classified as the 'manager', I had trouble filling in the forms and I hardly knew how to write an order for supplies, yet I was supposed to be the big boss, the head honcho in the bakery, but fortunately we had an administrator who helped me with the paperwork.

I learned to order flour only because Jean, the administrator's wife, helped me. I managed to keep things very simple, which I do even today. I have a real disability in lots of areas like that. Nowadays, my wife Christine says I "choose" not to be efficient with my paperwork, but today, of course, I have that freedom of choice, which I didn't have in Arnhem Land.

Being in Arnhem Land was like being in another world. Nowadays, I do visitations at the Beechworth Prison almost every week. The old prison is right in the middle of our town, but we now have a new one outside of town. When you go in there – it's also 'another world'.

There are lots of 'other worlds'.

ABORIGINES

I had no problem with the Aboriginal people because I've never been racist. Apart from the time I stabbed their son we got on very well with our Aboriginal neighbours in Tocumwal.

As children, we never saw our parents take exception to anyone because of their race. In fact, when Dad went to the pub he would often bring people home from every bloody nationality under the sun. And so, to me, the Aborigines were just another mob.

However, these people were black. They're not like dark-skinned urban or southern Aborigines, they're real *black!*. When I started on the job I was told, "Tom, the longer you stay here the whiter they get."

I started out thinking, "How can this happen?" But 15 months later they were all looking white to me, so I thought it was time to go because the Aborigines themselves wanted me to respect the differences between us.

MY LITTLE FLAT

Even though I got on with everyone up there, I never had any close friends. I'd come home every night to an empty flat – no TV, no radio, no phone, no books, but I read the paper when I could get one. When I was on my own I'd spend a bit of time gardening. I had banana trees, pineapples and other tropical plants. It was fairly unrewarding because there were only two seasons – the rainy season when everything was lush, and the dry season when the whole place looked like a red moonscape.

I lived in a little flat by myself. There was nothing in there much – just a bed, a table, and a fridge. I didn't really do anything in my flat, so my time in Maningrida was pretty boring, though it needn't have been. I mainly worked and slept. I didn't even read. I could have easily borrowed books, but I wasn't into reading. I got myself a second job instead, a part time job at the fast food place, the Hasty Tasty.

I saved quite a bit of money. Not many people up there worked two jobs, but I did. I would have worked a third job if I could.

They gave me a housekeeper, Marjorie, who couldn't speak a word of English, so I communicated with her through energetic sign language. Marjorie had very few facial expressions. She was a tribal Aborigine and she didn't really know anything about house cleaning. Marjorie would put *everything* in the fridge – the frying pan, the saucepan, the lot – but I didn't care what she did. What difference could it make? She'd have put the bloody radio in the fridge if I'd had one.

There were three flats in our block and Marjorie was supposed to clean them all. The other whitefellas wouldn't let her into theirs, so she only had my flat to clean – just wiping the vinyl floor and the table. When she wanted me, she sat outside my flat and just waited. Sometimes she'd wait for a long time without moving, then I'd come home and let her in. But there was nothing much for her to do except...get rid of the frogs!

I had a terrible fear of frogs and these bloody big things would come up through the septic system and sit inside the toilet bowl; ugly they were. I'd be desperately wanting to use the toilet but I couldn't face getting the frogs out, so Marjorie would get them out for me. I'd have to act like a frog before she'd understand what the hell I wanted. Then she'd come and calmly take the ugly thing away, so I could use the loo.

I mostly ate Campbell's Beef & Vegetable soup, bread, and not much else, I didn't cook proper meals because I busted my dentures twice on buffalo steaks in Maningrida and I didn't want to risk busting them again. I had to send them all the way to Darwin to get fixed, and it would take two weeks to get them back. Instead of yelling "bloody hurry up!" at the staff, I'd be going "Vruddy hully ug", and that doesn't get you anywhere.

The dentist would parcel them back to me in a cigarette packet. Of course, when they arrived I knew what was in there, so one day I said to Jim my baker: "Open that packet up ... Go on Jim...." Well, he got all thrilled about opening up the parcel – but he got a real shock when he saw it was my teeth!

To him it seemed so funny. He got so bloody excited that he started chasing Maurice and Solomon all around the bakehouse with what they called my 'toy teeth'.

They were so over-excited that I thought I was going to 'do' my teeth again.

BOMA BOMA

I always wanted to get into every female's pants; I really did. I was totally obsessed – but I didn't have the self-confidence, and it was worse than that because no one wanted me. I still didn't have a girlfriend, but I was friendly with Pauline Balding who lived in the flat behind my place (and coincidentally many years later she lived in Beechworth with her daughters until her recent move to London). Pauline was a kindergarten teacher. We have stayed friends all these years.

However, my self-image began to change because I was now a 'man', I had some authority and I was probably one of the youngest whitefellas on the settlement.

Story telling is an important form of entertainment in areas that don't have TV broadcasts and I had a few yarns in me. I'd go to parties and the people would say, "Tom, tell us about the time…" and away I'd go. I told them many childhood stories about the railways, Father Byrne, bats, suicides off the Red Bridge, the wild life and the mighty Murray River. I think my stories interested them because most of the white folk in Arnhem Land came from the city, whereas I was a country boy. There were a lot of educated people up there, plus labourers and builders, and they all seemed to enjoy listening to my stories. I was accepted by all levels of Maningrida society. In the light of my background I found that really strange.

I was accepted by the people who hated the Aborigines, I was accepted by those who liked them, and I was also accepted by the Aboriginal people.

I was invited to parties that excluded others. I was always welcome to join any group because no one found me a threat. Anyone could talk to me. I didn't express an opinion on many things and I don't now. There were a lot of political people there, but I wasn't one.

As for Aboriginal culture, I didn't ask too many questions, I just accepted it. Occasionally I'd get invited to a burial or a circumcision ceremony. It was no big deal to me, when I was 20.

The Aborigines didn't call me 'Tom'; they called me 'Boma Boma'.

After about six months I said to Jim: "What does Boma Boma mean?"

He said it means, "You're mad".

They reckoned I was mad because I was the only guy on a government settlement who was always racing around. I'd yell: "Hurry up you buggers, bloody git this going!" I was in a hurry to bake the bread – the yeast wasn't waiting for anyone. I was always in a hurry, hurry, hurry. I was never one to sit around.

JIM, MAURICE, SOLOMON, MARGARET

Only black people worked for me and although I was in charge I didn't think of myself as having people 'under' me. I had staff of four – three bakers (two apprentices and Jim) plus 16-year old Margaret in the shop. Jim was really proud that he was a baker and he was good at it too. He had great baking skills.

We sold bread, cakes and pies – mainly to the Aboriginal people who especially loved fresh white bread. If I'd try to sell them yesterday's bread, they wouldn't want it; they only wanted it fresh – just like my customers today.

I can go crook and cut anybody with my tone of voice. One day I went crook at Margaret then I walked off and went back to the bakehouse. I was in there baking for a while when I noticed there were heaps of people in the shop – "Geez they're busy," I thought and I went up to check – but Margaret wasn't there.

"Where's Margaret?" I said to the customers.

Nobody said anything, but they all looked 'that way'.

'That way' was the direction where the white people's houses were. There was only one Aboriginal house in that area: the blacktracker's place. He was the policeman's assistant, and I figured that's where I'd find Margaret, judging by the way everyone was indicating with their eyes.

Years later they said to me: "Tom, no one else could have got away with what you did." I'm a mad bugger and this was another example of my breaching black and white protocol. I went straight over to the blacktracker's house and I said to his wife: "Where's Margaret?" She didn't say a word, but her eyes looked down the hallway so I burst into the bedroom.

I knew what the Aboriginals did when they hid - they would get under the bed. So I stuck my hand under the bed, grabbed a skinny leg (because Margaret's legs were really skinny) pulled, and out came their bloody pet kangaroo. I was ******* wild!

I looked around, and Mrs Blacktracker was still standing there watching, so I shoved my arm back under the bed a second time, I got it right this time, I grabbed Margaret's leg, pulled her out and said: "Get back to bloody work!" She went quietly back, and everything was back to normal again.

Jim, Maurice and Solomon were buggers when they slept in. When they didn't show up, I would jump onto my Suzuki 175cc motor bike and tear up to the tin hut where Jim slept. (His hut is still there today, just a square box with no windows and one door.) I'd go there early in the morning, feel around in the dark, grab a leg and pull. *Out! Out!* I could hardly breathe in this place, it was musty and smoky and I'd often pull out the wrong person. So I'd let him or her go, stick the arm back in and pull out another one until I got Jim.

I'm a mad bugger because I knew that Jim had been locked up in Fanny Bay Jail for killing someone. Way before my time, he'd speared someone in a tribal war. He couldn't have been in jail long, because he would never have survived. A jail sentence would have broken his spirit, for fulfilling what was in his eyes, tribal law. Tactfully, I was always threatening to send him back to Fanny Bay. Fortunately, he didn't have a spear handy and he always laughed.

I used to get Solomon and Maurice the same way, "Git out of bed you buggers! Git to work!" Maurice lived in a whitefella's-style of house which was off the ground, but sometimes I'd still have to fossick around to find him. Solomon was a bit shorter and a little bit plumper, and harder to pull out. At times he would run away from me, the little bugger.

Although we weren't always quite on the same side, Jim and me were a real 'team'. I'd pillion him to work on my Suzuki. I don't know how he hung on, but he had incredible balance. He would hang on like an octopus, limbs waving in the air and legs kicking at the camp dogs that would chase after us. Before we'd take off, Jim would usually grab a big stick to beat off the dogs as we rode out. Jim would be swinging his stick at the dogs even though there was an unspoken rule that you weren't allowed to hurt the dogs.

One day I was running late because Jim had slept in. We were gunning along the road and I was really angry. I'm not a good rider and all of a sudden a bloody dog ran out in front of us and – bang! - I hit it. Jim and I both left the seat, bounced back on and when we looked back we realised that we had killed the dog. We sure weren't going to bloody stop. That would be looking for heaps of trouble.

People couldn't understand how I got away with so much. Bursting into places, killing dogs, yelling, screaming and carrying on. Years later they said to me: "Tom, we can't understand how you got away with behaving like that." The answer is, I got away with it because they knew I was committed. I was there to do my job. I wasn't there to rip them off. I would have done the same to whitefellas if they were bloody late, and the Aboriginal people could see that. They could see I had no issues with the Aborigines, or Labor-voting school teachers (we had lots of them), displaced bureaucrats or anybody else. I just treated everybody the same.

I was at a party one day and I was introduced to a guy called Howdy. I greeted him and said: "Howdy, what's your real name?"

Then I felt Merv's hand on my shoulder, pulling me aside. He said: "Tom, don't ever ask anybody their real name in the Territory." I got the picture.

When Jim's brother died, he had to take on his brother's wife – that meant that Jim now had two wives. Next, another girl who'd been promised to him came of age, and he didn't want a third. She was totally tribal. She couldn't speak a word of English. I said: "Jim! Give her to me! Give her to me!" Of course, he couldn't give her to me. That was against the rules.

THE HAND JOB

I'd go crook at Jim for putting too much oil into the oven when he lit it because it would explode. One day I was there lighting the bloody oven and next minute BOOM, it just knocked me over backwards and blew me straight out the back door. Any time I go crook at anybody else for burning cakes or burning pies, sure as bloody hell I'll do it three times worse the next day or the next week, so I try not to go crook because I put the moz on myself when I do.

The baker before me had ordered a moulder from Adelaide. It travelled safely all the way to Darwin, but when it arrived on the docks it got dropped. So they ordered another one four months before I arrived.

After I was there eight months, finally the big day arrived, and the heavy old dough moulder (which was 40 years old) arrived on the barge and we put it into the bakehouse. It rumbled and made a lot of noise, and Jim, Maurice and Solomon knew that machine was going to kill us all. They were pretty scared of The Beast.

The moulder was on one side of the bakehouse and the power plug was on the other. We stretched a long lead across the room, and we ran the dough through the moulder that day. Everything was going well – we moulded and did our bread, and then I thought for safety reasons I should show Jim and Maurice how dangerous a moulder can be. I said, "Don't ever clean it like this" and I took the guard off the top and I showed them what not to do. I said: "Don't ever clean it like this, it's too danger..." and the next minute *sshoonk*! I put my bloody hand in the machine. There I was, so stupid, telling them don't ever take the guard off – and I took the stupid thing off!

Well, my hand went in the machine and I let out a wild scream, it was like running your fingers through a steel wringer of an old washing machine. My hand went right in – and I started screaming, "Turn it off! Turn the bloody power off!" Screaming! Screaming! And instead of pulling out the lead, Jim, Maurice and Solomon were so terrified that they all ran for the door, all trying to get out at the same time. Their courage is imprinted in my memory forever. They wouldn't turn off the machine; they ran for their lives instead! I taught them all right. They never ever took the top off again.

Next minute there were people coming in from everywhere and someone turned the power off at last. I ended up getting a trip with the Flying Doctor and I spent 12 days in a hospital in Darwin, with a drip in my left hand.

BACK IN TOC

Although Mum said she didn't miss me, I think all my family were proud of me. I was very lonely.I didn't get any news of home. I wrote to them, but they didn't write back and phoning wasn't worth the effort. There was only one public radio phone on the settlement, and talking on it was too much like hard work, which was made even more complicated by the fact that my parents didn't have a phone.

I had left my old Volkswagen with my parents at Toc, so I wrote to Mum and said: "If you get your licence Mum, you can use my car until I get back." So she went and got her licence. She was never a good driver. When I came back from the Territory and took the car back, she was really upset with me because my parents didn't have the money to buy another one. But in time my brothers, my sister and me did keep them in cars – old cars, EH Holdens, Cortinas and cars like that.

WHAT'S A SLAB?

A barge from Darwin delivered supplies every 10 days. When I got there, the guy next door (who organised the supplies) said, "How many slabs do you want Tom?"

I said: "What's a slab, Bert?"

He said: "24 cans of beer."

I said to him: "How many do you get?"

He said: "I get 10" – a slab a day – *shit!*"

I was very tight, I didn't like wasting my money on alcohol and I said, "I'll get two slabs" – and by the end of the 10 days I used to sell one back to Bert. Even so, I'd have a hard time getting through one whole slab over 10 days.

I was never a beer drinker and I didn't get into the grog. Lots of people did, but I had a goal. I got paid a good wage every week, which I'd put aside and watch my bank balance grow. I wanted to buy my own business as soon as possible.

NEW GUINEA

When I was 19 I fell in love with Mary Kelly, a nurse from Rutherglen, Victoria. At the time I was doing my apprenticeship in Albury. At night a few of the rowdy bakers used to get onto the bakery phone and ring the Nurse's Home. They'd chat up the nurses but I was too shy to talk. They'd call out to me, "Tom, come and talk to the nurses," and I'd usually say 'no'. But one night I got talking to Mary Kelly and we made a date, went out and of course I fell madly in love with her – which was pretty normal. I'd fall in love with any woman who'd talk to me.

I went out with Mary for a while, then she broke it off and left me totally devastated. I'd almost forgotten about her until she wrote to me when I was in the Territory. Mary contacted me because she was going to New Guinea to meet up with her brother at Mount Hagan, and I said I'd like go over to.

I bought the ticket and showed up at Darwin Airport. I didn't know you needed a passport to travel overseas until one of the airport officials said to me: "You can't just hop on the plane without a passport." So I called the boss of Maningrida, Glen Bagshaw, who placed a phone call and sent me to a politician's office in Darwin, where I waited all day until late. The plane was leaving that evening and I ended up getting on it thanks to the politician and thanks to Glen. I remained in New Guinea for about three weeks.

While I was there, Mary's brother, Peter and his wife asked me to make some bread. I'm not a great baker and it exploded in the oven! It was good bread but it was all in pieces.

There were hardly any white people and about 25,000 natives in this valley above Mount Hagan. When I was there it rained for a short burst every day. I had some great times up there with the natives. They held a big community sport's day and I climbed up this greasy pole. The idea was to take turns knocking each other off - and the natives belted the shit out of me. No other white person was silly enough to get up there, but I did. The natives loved it. They belted hell out me, and I belted them back. They nearly knocked my head off a couple of times. It was great fun.

I BECOME TOM O'TOOLE

Mary and I left New Guinea together and we flew to Albury. I stayed at her place in Rutherglen for a week during which time I bought a block of land at Wahgunyah – a tiny little town out of Corowa – which has never gone ahead. It was a real bummer of a buy, but I was really lucky because I bought and sold it at a good price, it's still a vacant block today.

I was sitting in the solicitor's office doing the paperwork and on impulse I asked him, "How much does it cost to change your name?"

He said: "$23."

I said: "Change it."

I was sick of being called 'Dickhead' and 'Shovel' because of my name: Tom Toole. I said, "Change it to O'Toole" which means 'son of Toole'.

It was the best $23 I've ever spent, but it didn't change what was inside of me; I was still an angry young man.

When I returned to Maningrida some guy yelled out, "Hey, Dickhead" and I said: "You can't bloody call me that any more, I've changed my name and I'm not a Toole anymore."

He looked a bit shocked and said: "What did your parents say?"

He looked even more surprised when I said: "I haven't told 'em."

Mary dropped me again during those holidays. All over - finished. But that was okay, because I had seen a business for sale in Yarrawonga, Victoria. I went back up to the Territory and I handed in my notice because I knew that if I didn't get out, I'd be there forever. And I wanted to get into my own business.

GOUGH

In December 1972 there was a change of Government. Gough Whitlam became the new Prime Minister of Australia and there were big celebrations in Maningrida where there were lots of Labor supporters.

It didn't really worry me one way or the other because I'm not political. But I thought Whitlam made things much better for the Aboriginal people because they weren't bound to live in settlements any more. They could go back to their land if they wanted to.

Whitlam also announced his decentralisation policy, part of which was his intention to develop Albury-Wodonga as a regional centre. As a result, the blocks of land I'd bought for $2000 in Albury (before going to Maningrida) instantly tripled in value. Somebody got onto me and offered me double, and I sold them.

It sounded good, but it wasn't much of a deal for me because I didn't know what my blocks were really worth. Prices were far more inflated than I realised; being on the northern tip of Australia was like being in another country.

CHANGED MY LIFE

I saw some incredible sights in Arnhem Land. Sometimes I went out with archaeologists, who took me on four-wheel drive trips. One day we went searching for a known waterfall that was in a valley that had only ever been entered once before by whites. Not even Aborigines lived in this valley any more. There I saw rock paintings of Spanish soldiers, Tasmanian tigers, sailing ships plus many different types of burial situations – bodies buried in caves, hollow logs and in rock crevices.

But that was exceptional, most of my time in Maningrida was spent working two jobs. I wasn't a little bush boy anymore, like I was on the Murray. I didn't even swim up there; there's too many bloody crocs, sharks and stingers. You could only swim in the fresh-water holes and that wasn't too often because they were way out of town. No, there wasn't too much to do if you were a single guy.

There was no pub, just a nightly Happy Hour for the Aborigines who were allowed three stubbies each per night.

They showed good teamwork – they'd form groups of three where two wouldn't have any, and one would have nine, and so each drinker would get pissed every third night.

My 15 months in Maningrida changed my life. I felt I was a real somebody at last. Before that, because of my low self-worth, I saw myself as always being invisible.

But in this environment I felt very comfortable because dress wasn't important, shoes weren't important, speech wasn't important. I've never had good speech; there were lot of words I couldn't pronounce properly. Plus my manner has always been pretty bloody direct. When I went back into white society, I'd shout, "Hurry up, you bastards!" and my staff would say things back like, "You're not talking to yer blackfellas now!" But being black had nothing to do with it, I would treat whitefellas exactly the same way. I would yell and scream at all people equally.

However, I now felt heaps better about myself. I'd changed my name, I'd managed a successful business, I'd been overseas and I wasn't a bloody nobody any more. I was Tom O'Toole, the baker.

I was also beginning to realise that a baker was a great thing to be. The Maningrida Bakery was a cornerstone of the whole community. I was well respected, I got invitations to all sorts of places and I was earning good money. On visiting Maningrida, dignitaries came out of their way to meet my bakers, and I'm pretty sure that Margaret Fulton, the celebrity cook, came up there too. Politicians and others were keen to meet us - and here I was a *baker!*

I feel the same applies today; I'm still pretty well accepted by all sorts of different groups. With my public speaking I sometimes talk to doctors, funeral directors, secretaries, CEOs, professionals and I also talk to people in prison. I got my first taste of that cross-section of acceptance at Maningrida.

I think they accept me because I don't get on my soapbox and preach. Who am I to judge anyone? Maybe I learned that off my Dad; I'm not sure. He accepted everybody. Poor people, rich people, he could talk to them all. He'd even go to Church and talk to the people there.

My Dad was proud. He would stand up straight. He always wore a coat and tie (even though they came from St Vincent de Paul stores). I can't recall him ever buying a new piece of clothing. He never had any money to waste on new clothes, yet he always looked good. My Dad used to say to me, "Just because we're poor, we don't have to look poor."

The Aboriginal people at Maningrida were also proud. They too didn't need new clothes to feel good about themselves.

We were the odd ones out. It was their language, their rules and their land.

GOIN' HOME

I knew if I didn't get out of Arnhem Land I'd be there forever and that I probably would have ended up marrying an Aboriginal girl. I was falling in love with lots of them, which wasn't smart because that sort of behaviour wasn't permitted.

For example, one bloke - an educated Christian guy - got involved with an Aboriginal girl after he'd only been up there for a few weeks. A white lady dobbed him in to the administrators who put him on the next plane out – leaving that very day. They told him that if he didn't get on that afternoon flight, they could not guarantee his safety. He may well have been speared.

And so I left knowing with certainty that I was going to use my capital and my management experience to start a business in north-east Victoria.

Some people might wonder, how could I have the confidence to go into business when I couldn't even read a bank statement?

I didn't worry about the 'how?' - I just *knew*.

I left the Territory and went straight into my first business at 21 in Yarrawonga. But that's another chapter.

ARNHEM LAND REVISITED

In 1999, Christine and I took the family back to Arnhem Land after 27 years. We had a wonderful time. It was great to catch up with old friends.

I met up with Jim who is now an elder of his tribe. He's recently got himself a brand new home but he usually prefers to hang out in the tin hut that I knew so well. I didn't dare ask how many wives he now has!

Maurice is now also a leader in his tribe. He wrapped his arms around me and explained to Christine: "Tom was a very hard man but very good; he taught us many things." He said: "More people need to be like Tom. Today I can help my people because Tom helped me."

They remembered me after 27 years! And even though I was an angry bugger, Maurice thanked me.

He said: "No one comes back and visits: no one."

They were so pleased that I came back.

CHAPTER FIVE

IT'S HARD, IT'S HARD!

Life is either a daring
adventure or nothing.
Helen Keller

Yarrawonga is a Victorian border town, located on the edge of Lake Mulwala. Its name comes from the Aboriginal word 'Cormorant's nesting place'. The 6000 hectare lake was cleared by volunteer axemen in the 1930s, and it is this and the Murray River that attracts visitors to the town. Mown lawns and willow trees slope down to the lake where water activities abound – water skiing, sailboarding, boating, swimming, and distant memories of paddle ships.

In the very centre of Yarrawonga, close to the Shire Hall, the Royal Mail Hotel, the Terminus, the Chronicle newspaper, the Central Café and the Anzac Memorial, is 65 Belmont Street - the site of my first bakery, which backs onto Hobel Street. I lived onsite between the bakehouse and the shop. Like my Maningrida dwelling, I only had the very basic essentials: one bedroom and another little room. It didn't have a kitchen, and I built the shower.

I bought the Yarrawonga business while I was still in Arnhem Land. I got my old boss Frank Sinnett from Albury to do me a favour, and go and check it out. He said: "It's okay."

The business cost $10,000 and I paid in cash but I didn't buy the premises, I just took over the lease and paid for goodwill. The machinery was virtually non-existent, the oven was wood-fired, but I got caught really badly because the previous owner had signed a contract with Sunicrust in which he agreed that the bakery wouldn't produce sliced bread. And as everybody knows, sliced bread is every baker's stock-in-trade.

I was stitched up.

ANY MACHINERY?

Over the year and a quarter that I was in Maningrida, Sunicrust had been buying up lots of independent bakeries over regional Victoria and southern New South Wales. Their strategy was to close them down, destroy the equipment and supply all the towns from one central bakery in Wodonga, which was huge.

When I came back I saw that many of the Wise Brothers' bakeries had shut down. These shut-downs were so sudden and so dramatic that bowls were left with the ingredients still in them. Trays were still covered in flour. Sunicrust brought in lots of other machinery and I noticed they were using the old Albury bakery premises for storage.

Frank was now working for Sunicrust and because I desperately needed tins and trays, I said to him: "Is there any machinery left?"

He said: "Well Tom, we're not allowed to sell it. It's got to go to the scrap metal dealer."

I was shocked: "You mean the moulders, ovens, mixers...?"

"Yep – the lot," said Frank. "They're coming in with sledge hammers and smashing the machinery so no one else can use it. They've done the same thing with the flour mills."

I said: "That's a real waste Frank, someone could be making good use of that equipment."

Frank looked at me and smiled: "Tom get in there – just once. Get what you can fit in your car and we'll leave it at that."

That's all the encouragement I needed! I stripped the guts out of my Volkswagen – I didn't tell Frank this – and I loaded it up with tins, bowls, trays, even a dough break ... heaps of stuff. So much that, to get out the driveway, I ended up ripping off both of my exhaust pipes because my car was so loaded up.

And then, just before closing up, I spotted Frank's solid timber desk. I always wanted a proper desk, so I said to him, "Can I buy it?"

He said: "Sure." He was allowed to sell it because it wasn't machinery, and he let me have it cheap.

So I had this flash desk in this falling down old bakery in Yarrawonga. Wow, I was a business man at last!

SAD SANDWICHES

Although I came back from Arnhem Land with renewed self-confidence, I still suffered incredible fears and I found it almost impossible to mix in society. I tried going to church but I found that very cliquey. No one wanted to talk to me.

I think being a Roman Catholic is the greatest religion in the world – you can muck up all week, go to confession, and then start all over again! One thing's for sure, they don't hassle you or try to convert you or even talk to you. They wouldn't talk to me.

I was lonelier than I ever was in Maningrida. Every day I went to the café and bought a corned beef and salad sandwich for lunch. I found it really objectionable that they put all their prices up during the tourist season. Here I was – a regular and a local – and they charged me bloody tourist's prices. I found that really strange. However, I should thank the old Continental Café for that lesson, because it's something I've learned never to do. I've never lifted my prices during the holiday season.

Hoping someone would talk to me, I'd sometimes wander down to the Royal Mail Hotel for a counter lunch. Maybe I'd have a beer or two but I preferred lemon squash or milk shakes. But no one talked to me there either. Looking back, I realise I wasn't really approachable. *If you want a friend, be a friend.* I never had any friends in Yarrawonga.

I didn't go back to Tocumwal much. Some of my family were still in Toc but I'd moved on. There was nothing there for me any more. I don't think anyone even recognised me when I came back.

ALONE AGAIN

It wasn't just the church and the pub, I found the whole town very bloody cliquey, but it was probably me. I often roamed the streets without shoes. I was missing Arnhem Land and my Aboriginal friends. I didn't really want to be a loner.

I almost cried myself to sleep some nights, I just wanted to go back to Jim, Maurice and Solomon in Maningrida – because it was easy there. I felt at home among the Aboriginal people, but I found it very difficult to mix in white society.

Now that I owned my own bakery, I was supposedly a 'business man', yet I had no idea how to act. I've never talked 'business language', 'business buzz words' and all that – *especially* not when I was 21. My vocabulary was a lot bloody smaller than it is now.

However, the potential to make money in Yarrawonga was terrific, though I had no idea how to capitalise on that. There were 3500 locals as well as an influx of 20,000 tourists, and all of them had money to spend on cakes and pies.

CHRISTMAS EVE PANIC

On my first Christmas Eve there, one of my girls took sick. That left me short-staffed in the shop.

Then the other girl said, "I've got to go now, I've got a doctor's appointment", and I was left all alone with a roomful of hungry customers, all wanting to give me money.

I tried to serve them one at a time, but there were too many. I found myself thinking about who to serve next? Who's been waiting longest? How am I going to handle the numbers? And then I started to panic and in the end I just said: "Come behind the counter, help yourselves and just leave the money on the till."

I couldn't cope. It was a terrible experience.

Today I say to my staff: "Just serve one customer at the time, that's all you can do." I learned that lesson when I panicked that Christmas Eve.

BUSINESS IS NO GOOD

Because I was such a loner, I had no people skills. I also had no business skills.

I've never been a person who would ask for help and I was making a big mistake in using the previous owner's accountant and it wasn't working at all. Fortunately, when my bank manager said, "change your accountant", I listened.

And then the truth started coming out, my new accountant said: "Tom, this business is no good." No matter what I did, it would never turn a healthy profit largely because of the restraint agreement with Sunicrust.

Another problem was that when I took over, the previous owner's prices were so low that it had ceased to be viable. He knew what he was doing – he was the good guy who kept prices down and then sold out; and I was the bad guy bought in and lifted the prices.

Even when I bumped my prices up, my profit margin was still too low because of inflation. So I was pretty dejected, and that's when I ended up reading *The Power Of Positive Thinking*, and I'll get to that soon.

I employed five people: three on the counter plus two bakers. One of them was a guy called Harry, and the other one was the previous owner's brother. The owner told me not to employ him because he was an alcoholic. At that time I didn't know what a bloody alcoholic was – I just knew him as a great baker.

SEAGULL MANAGEMENT

Yelling and screaming, that's how I ran the Yarrawonga business. I was a real seagull manager – I'd fly in, crap on everyone, make lots of noise and then leave. I'd be all right but they'd be devastated.

```
      I ran all my businesses
      like that until I was 32.
      Yelling and screaming was
          the only way I knew.
      I never said, 'please' or
        'thank you' to anybody.
      I reckoned being nice was
        a bloody waste of time.
```

I didn't bother to do any advertising; I just opened the shop hoping the people would buy. And they didn't.

I'd think: "Why don't all these thousands of tourists come in here?" I couldn't understand the problem. And today I see lots of shops with people standing behind their lonely counters hoping customers will walk in their doors. I felt trapped behind the counter. It was like being in prison. I'd think: "I could be doing something worthwhile like gardening, swimming or washing my clothes, instead I'm standing behind this bloody counter doing nothing except hoping someone will come into my shop and buy something."

And when they'd come in, I'd resent the bastards!

IT'S HARD

The first book I ever read was a Prayer Book from which my sister Betty taught me to read when I was 10.

After that I never read any real books at all. I'd only read 'stick' books - Playboy and the sort of stuff where I only had to look at the pictures. I was young and silly. But I did get around to reading one proper book.

I was sitting outside the bakehouse on a milk crate feeling dejected and lonely when an elderly man came along, his name was Russ Green, and he was a Bakel's rep.

Russ said: "Tom, what are you looking so *happy* for?"

I said: "It's hard! It's hard! It's all too hard."

He said: "You've got to stop reading them Playboys!"

I said: "You don't understand Russ, I mean the business is hard. The bakery isn't making any money. I can't make it work!"

Russ told me to read *The Power Of Positive Thinking* by Norman Vincent Peale, which I bought from the Yarrawonga Newsagency.

This was the first book I can remember ever buying. I'd read heaps of comics, but I can't say I'd ever read a book before then. It was a positive book and I was a pretty negative guy. It made me so positive that I bought another business straight away and then I tried to sell the Yarrawonga bakery - but I couldn't.

POSITIVE MCINTOSH THINKING

I was sitting outside the bakery reading all this positive stuff when Keith McIntosh and his family came to visit. Keith and his brother

Bernie owned the Ideal Café (now the Beechworth Bakery). Keith told me that he wanted to get out; he was desperate. We sat on the foreshore of Lake Mulwala under a willow tree and talked about his problems with the café and I said, "I want to buy it." But I had no money left.

I'd first met Keith in Beechworth when I was 17 doing my apprenticeship with Baker Boy. He was nine years older than me, a baker by trade, but at the time he was a psych nurse doing a bit of moonlighting in the bakery.

Keith was a man when I was only a boy. He befriended me, took me exploring the bush; we had lots of laughs together. Some years ago Christine and I had an opal mine in Lightning Ridge where we got a few opals, we've travelled the Birdsville Track, the Oodnadatta Track, Uluru, and in 2003 we drove to Cape York on a 4-wheel drive-only track in my 1930 A-Model Ford bakery van with no doors - 8000 kms at an average speed of 50 kph. A lot of people reckoned we wouldn't make it. We were pretty silly, but we got home. Keith was my friend way back then and he still is today.

Nowadays, he does sampling in the Beechworth Bakery and he tells everyone: "I'm Tom's friend. I've known him for years. I've been his best man three times."

He's a bullshit-artist. I've only been married twice (and that's enough).

IDEAL BEECHWORTH

Years before, I used to come gold panning in Beechworth with my brother-in-law, Allan Friar. I always liked Beechworth; to me there was always "gold in them hills". One day I'll be buried in Beechworth, but not for a long long time.

In 1824, explorers Alexander Hume and William Hovell set out to explore the south, beyond the known settlements. Their diary entries show they passed through the foothills where Beechworth is today and they loved the look of the place. In the middle of the 19th century it was the most populated town in north east Victoria, with a population of 20,000 in 1857, almost half of whom were gold miners. Some people believe that in the 1850s it rivalled Melbourne as the capital of Victoria.

Chinese gold miners, legendary bushrangers (Ned Kelly and Harry Powers), the ill-fated Captain Robert O'Hara Burke (Burke & Wills), gold, gold and more gold, are the reasons why the history of Beechworth runs deep. Other famous names include Dame Jean McNamara, 'The Dame' (the doctor who treated my wife Christine, and who is buried in the Beechworth Cemetery), and more recently pole vaulter Emma George, who broke all the world records.

In the 1850s, the village of Melbourne began transforming itself into an important city. So did Beechworth, which built most of its significant buildings in the same decade – the hospital, the benevolent asylum, the Beechworth Jail, Beechworth's first schools, hotels and churches, the Post Office built in granite and the 14th Masonic Lodge in the Colony. *Go Beechworth!*

In the same decade, Camp Street was surveyed, divided into lots, and auctioned. The first owner of the bakery land was general storekeeper Charles Williams who bought the block in 1853. Under the ownership of its third owner, David Dunlop, 1871 marks the first time the site was used as a bakery. The second storey was constructed about 1910.

Through its 150-year history, it was at first a shoe and boot shop, then the site of Byrne's Tearooms, a confectioner, a pastry shop and a café.

Ned Kelly must have known the shop reasonably well. One of the most famous Ned Kelly photographs was taken at James Bray's studio in Camp Street, handy to my shop. And James Ingram, of Ingram's Booksellers and Stationers, directly across the road from the bakery, often reminisced about Ned's visits to his shop. We can only surmise that Kelly probably crossed the road, and walked past or into my shop.

Whereas the Beechworth of the 1850s had seven times its current population, in the 1950s it was a town facing extinction. The town gardens were wild and overgrown and the line of granite Government buildings in Ford Street were neglected. Government bureaucrats might have called Beechworth 'insignificant' but I thought it was beautiful: the kind of town I was proud to call 'home'.

Forget the banks, it was Keith and Bernie's mother who lent me the money to buy her sons out. I bought the Ideal Café in partnership with my sister Betty and my brother-in-law Allan because I needed someone to balance books for me and to make up for my other inadequacies.

In 1974, we paid a total of $27,000 for the Ideal Café with Allan and Betty buying a half share. We then had to buy the freehold.

We all lived above the bakery, Betty and Allan, their three little kids: Alana, Dianne and Andrew, and me.

So I now had two businesses – one in Yarrawonga (that I didn't want) and another in Beechworth (that I loved). I used to travel between the two in my Austin 1800. When I blew it up (because I'm hopeless with cars) I would hitch-hike between the two towns holding a cardboard box in which I carried my books and papers. I carried everything around in a cardboard box until 1995 when Christine bought me a briefcase. I was so embarrassed, why carry a briefcase when a box will do?

MAD MAX

One day I was working away in the bakehouse and Max Cooper came in and asked for a job. Max had a chequered past; he told me this while I was cooking hamburgers. I couldn't think of much to say, so I said: "Are you hungry?"

He said: "Yes." So I handed him something to eat and he started sticking food into his mouth like a madman. He wasn't hungry, he was starving!

I said: "Okay, you can start tomorrow." He worked for me for years.

Max was a very talented baker who taught me heaps. The only trouble was, he'd forget everything we had done the day before.

I'd say: "How did we do this yesterday?"

He'd blank out and say: "I dunno."

While he was working for me Max was actually certified insane. It wasn't me who sent him mad. Now, to be certified insane is very difficult, because you need to convince three doctors, which Max managed with ease. I got Max back after he was certified. Every 10 days they'd show up and give him a needle which would virtually turn him into a zombie.

Max had an invisible mate who he brought to work with him every day and he talked to him all the bloody time, which I didn't mind. Then he'd go to the pub and buy two beers, one for himself and one for the invisible mate. Max was as mad as a two-bob watch, but he made me look good.

I tended to employ mostly people with living problems, alcoholics and maddies.

Max once stood outside the Westpac Bank in Beechworth, waited until the bank manager's wife came out and then pissed on her leg.

The police weren't too happy with Max. They were sure he terrorised women on his way to work at 3 am.

The police would ask me: "What time was Max at work last night?" And I'd say: "He arrived at five to three."

Well, the women he'd scared would only have an approximate idea of the time. They'd say, "I was woken at 3 am," but I'd confirmed Max 's alibi: that he was at the Bakery five minutes before. So, of course, there was always that doubt and the police would always say to me: "We're gonna get him Tom, we're gonna get him."

Last Christmas I saw Max back in the street, standing outside the newsagent, still talking to himself. I was surprised (and very pleased) he was still alive.

YARRAWONGA GOODBYE

Meanwhile, back in Yarrawonga, it was open combat: Home Pride and Sunicrust, two big wholesale bakeries, started a price war and they were selling bread down to 10 cents a loaf. But I ignored them. I've never got into a price war and I still won't get into price wars today.

I only had the Yarrawonga bakery for two years before selling it, and I didn't make money on the sale. Looking back, I don't suppose that really mattered because even though I whinged and complained about the bloody place, Yarrawonga is actually a very good town with excellent business possibilities, and lots to do for visitors, though it had nothing for me.

I sold the Yarrawonga Bakery to a guy who ended up going broke. He was a 'returnee' – a returned soldier from Vietnam with a war loan. I was so desperate to get out that I gave him vendor finance but, unfortunately, I was the second mortgagee and he just walked out and left it.

I went to see my solicitor who said, "Tom, being the second mortgagee isn't worth a damn thing", so I chucked the papers straight into the solicitor's rubbish bin. When I rang the Army up about the money he owed them, they weren't interested in pursuing their debt, which meant that despite being the No 2 mortgagee, I was literally the front-runner. The Army told me: "A couple of thousand dollars is too little for us to bother with." The Army wasn't interested in chasing up the small stuff and if I hadn't chucked those papers out I could have got my money back, because no one was doing anything with the shop.

That bakehouse stayed locked up for years, and all the time I was thinking: "Geez, I'd like to get my hands on some of them tins and trays."

BEECHWORTH BAKERY & MILK BAR

Together, my sister Betty and her husband Allan Friar worked the counter and the books at the Ideal Café, while I ran the bakery. I was the baker, Allan was the brains. We gradually built up the business as well as the equipment. One time I drove to Darling Point in the Riverina; I bought an old single arm mixer from a bakery which had closed down. I also bought a little moulder. After a while I put a bigger oven in and started to bake bread.

We changed the name from the Ideal Café to 'The Beechworth Bakery & Milk Bar'. We sold bread, lollies, ice creams, fruit, vegies, groceries, milk and cigarettes. It was a real Mum & Dad corner store operation.

When I bought it, I got out of Yarrawonga and moved to Beechworth straight away.

"The Beechworth Bakery is marvellous," said Mum. "But you should have seen it when it was the Ideal Café. I worked there when Tommy bloody first took it over. Tom did the cooking and everything. Betty and Allan were there with him too – they all lived upstairs. Tom's got the tea-rooms up there now. He's really turned it into something, he's put tables upstairs and sells cakes up the top."

BELONGING IN BEECHWORTH

I loved Beechworth for lots of reasons, and one of them was because there was a mental home there and the patients used to come into the shop. They made me feel I belonged in Beechworth. I didn't feel like a misfit any more, and because there were some strange looking people walking around, I felt right at home.

Misfits of society were walking the streets and they were accepted, like Connie, an elderly lady, who never had teeth and my staff would say, "Connie, it's Tom's birthday – go and give him a kiss!" She'd come running out the back and gave me a big kiss, "Happy Birthday Tom!" Kiss-kiss. The bastards, I was going to kill them!

There was also 'gold in them hills'. I was brought up in the flat country and I love the Murray, but I also love the Beechworth hills.

I worked every day in that bakery. I got very positive, I always knew there was something better for me, so I just worked. It was hard going because I started work at 3 am and the shop didn't shut until 9 pm. Sometimes I had to work the counter as well as the bakery. So I'd often go and have an afternoon sleep upstairs. We did a lot of hours and we were making good money. So I bought another block of land. Again, I couldn't get a bank loan.

HELLO CHRISTINE

To get among the women I had to go to the pub. I didn't have a car, I drank very little and I didn't smoke. The problem was that I couldn't hold up my end of a conversation in bars because I couldn't talk sex and sport. I knew nothing about either.

Then I met my future second wife Christine McAnanly at the Ideal Café.

Christine is a fifth generation Beechworthian. Her great-great grandfather Owen, and great-grandfather James were both miners. Her grandfather, Steve, was a drover. Her father Steve was a psych nurse and her Mum, Rose, was a domestic for the high school. Christine lived in the housing commission area on the north side of town near the jail, walking distance from the bakery.

Christine worked in the chemist shop which backed on to the bakery. The bakery was a parcel depot for the town, and Christine used to pick up the chemist's deliveries. She was 18, I was 23, and I was always interested in this quiet girl in mini-skirts. Though it was unusual for me to go to the pub, one night in the lounge at the Tanswell's Commercial Hotel I got enough grog into me to have the courage to ask Christine if I could walk her home. We had a big pasho at her back door – wow! When I left her place that night I was on top of the world. She found me irresistible.

I went out with Christine for almost a year. I borrowed Allan's car and took her to Tocumwal to meet my folks. She was startled when Mum put the dinner plates on the floor for the dogs to lick clean!

I got tired of Christine after a while. She was too normal.

MINI-SKIRT ATTRACTION

I was pretty keen on a tall, attractive woman who used to sometimes come into the bakery. I would avoid going into the shop when she was there, because I was too nervous. The staff would tease me, saying: "Hey Tom, she's back!" This was Carol Doherty, whom I ended up marrying.

Carol had unbelievably long legs and was six feet tall. She used to wear really short mini-skirts and I'd climb into the lolly counter so that I could peer up her dress. Although none of the customers knew where I was, the staff did. They'd say to me, "She's got a wedding ring on" and other times they'd say: "She hasn't."

One day, I was behind the deli fridge checking out her legs – and I suddenly got game. I sprang up and frightened her. She didn't know anyone was there.

I appeared out of nowhere and said: "Are you married or not?"

She said: "Sort of."

I didn't know what 'sort of' meant, so I disappeared again.

A few days later I met Carol in the pub and after I'd had a fair bit to drink I got really confident, and I asked her: "Can I give you a ride home?" She was separated from her husband at the time, so she said: "All right." I didn't own a car, so I had to quickly negotiate with Allan to borrow his EH Holden and we hopped in and talked in the car.

I just about had her talked into coming up to my flat, but because I'd had a bit much to drink, I spewed out the window instead. So she didn't come up that night.

The next day I was riding my pushbike and I met her up the street and I said: "Can I give you a ride home?" She said: "Sure."

I said: "Hop on."

I was dinking her, but she was so tall, her feet were hitting the bloody ground. She was living in a caravan at the time. Within a week she moved in with me.

THE HUSBAND

A lot of Carol's gear was still in Wangaratta where her husband lived, and one day she said: "Let's go get it." Well, I was a bit scared of that, I was scared of husbands. So I went to see the same solicitor who had advised me to chuck my mortgagee papers in the bin. I checked with him and he said: "Tom, don't do it. If you get caught you'll go for breaking and entry." But I went against his advice.

I drove to Wangaratta with Carol and arrived at a time when she knew her husband would be out. She got in and I followed. I felt really uneasy. I felt his presence in the room the whole time. I could smell him. He was a smoker, so the whole place smelled of husband. When I saw his cigarettes lying on the coffee table, I thought, "Shit! He's still around!" It was like robbing the place.

Yet Carol was so confident, she grabbed the frying pan, all her clothes, sheets, speakers, she grabbed this and that, walked out, closed the door, packed everything into the EH and headed back to Beechworth with me.

Two days later, I was in my flat having my afternoon sleep in this guy's red satin sheets, which Carol had told me were hers.

To get into my flat was a bit of maze. You had to go through a trapdoor in an alleyway, then through another door and up a steep staircase. There were three locked doors between my flat and the street but that day, I mustn't have locked the doors.

Because of my early starts I slept during the day, while Carol worked across the road at the Westpac Bank. I always sleep with nothing on and suddenly I was awakened by a knock on the bedroom door, which was half open. I slowly came to the realisation that a guy was standing in my doorway. I thought it was one of my staff and I said: "Come in...." Then I recognised him from a photograph, "Shit, that's Carol's husband!"

Here I was naked in his satin sheets and all I could was think was, *bloody hell!*

He said: "I want some of my gear back."

I said: "All right, wait a sec." Well, I wasn't in a position to argue. I pulled my trousers on and said, "All right, whaddya want?"

He said: "My frying pan, my speakers, my riding boots..." He wanted this, he wanted that, he also wanted his engagement ring back. I loaded him right up and there he was standing at the top of the stairs. I thought: "I'll give him a push and that'll be the end of him." But I didn't and off he went.

Then Carol came back after work and I said: "Your husband called. He wanted the frying pan and...." Wow! Did she go off! (And she didn't go off too often.)

"Did you give it to him? Bloody hell! That was *my* frying pan!"

Oh geez I was in the shit! I went over to the hardware shop and bought another frying pan straight away. What else could I do?

Then I got into trouble some more because Carol reckoned the frying pan wasn't the problem – it was the speakers that she was mad about. I couldn't win.

FROGS & YABBIES & GIRLFRIEND

I took Carol to Tocumwal to meet Mum and Dad. The meeting went okay until Carol wanted to take a shower. She went into the bathroom and the bath had a wet sugar bag lying in it. When she lifted the corner and saw all these frogs and yabbies under it she was a bit bloody shocked. She came out and said: "Bloody hell! What's in that?"

I calmly said "tree frogs" which was normal in our house. I added, "They're for Dad's fishing", and that was okay. That night she took a shower at my brother Terry's place – he had a little house up near the railway station after he and Wendy had got married.

When Carol and I came back a week later, the same thing happened again. She went to the bathroom to take a shower only to find the same frogs and the same yabbies in the same bath. My Dad hadn't got around to going fishing and she said to me, "Don't your parents use the bath?"

I was a bit embarrassed, because I've never known my father to have a bath. I've seen my mother have a shower in the summer. She'd stand there fully clothed under the shower to help cool her down. But my Dad was Irish; he would wash, but never shower.

SORRY, CHRISTINE

Clearly I'd broken up with Christine. Broke her heart, I did. She was devastated and ended up going off to Melbourne where she became a nurse. For years, I never saw her again.

Carol and I lived together for a while. We bought a log cabin on Old Stanley Road, Beechworth. It was my first home and I loved it. I borrowed the money through the solicitor. Again, I couldn't get a bank loan. *How about that?*

Carol and I would fight a bit, but not enough to stop us getting married. We tied the knot in our Old Stanley Road home because we couldn't get married in a church. She'd been married before in the Darwin Cathedral but the Catholic Church wouldn't marry us because she'd been divorced. Carol lived through Cyclone Tracey in 1974 and stayed on. She was a really hard worker. She worked at the bank and, in time, she came and worked in the bakery.

My mad baker, Max Cooper, attended our wedding. Mum and Dad were there too. It was a little wedding. I got drunk and I told my mother what I thought of her. I told her all sorts of terrible things that I've forgotten. Geez, I was sick the next day.

I danced on the table. I put my little nephew's glasses on and bent them out of shape. Halfway through the ceremony, I took off my heeled shoes and instantly became shorter than my six feet tall wife. I ripped my tie off and did all that sort of stuff. It was funny, not too embarrassing, I think. They had to carry me to bed that night.

GO WEST

After three-and-a-half years in Beechworth, I said to Carol, "I've got to get out" because I thought I was going mad.

We ended up selling the bakery to two boxers, the 1972-73 Australian Light-Heavyweight Champion, Johnny van Gorkom (he boxed under the name Johnny Gorkom) and John Holt. We left money in the business until Johnny sold his house in Albury.

When I sold the business in Beechworth, Carol and I intended to ride around Australia on push bikes, but first I wanted to spend Christmas in Tocumwal, which we did and then we headed off along the Murray River to Deniliquin, Echuca, Robinvale and up to Mildura.

I nearly died of heat exhaustion. Carol and I were getting in practice because we wanted to ride across the Nullabor. We rode to Mildura, then down to Port Fairy, Warnambool, then back along the Great Ocean Road. When we got back Carol rang up her family in Western Australia and found out that her father had suffered a heart attack, so she hopped on a plane and flew home.

I bought a Toyota Corona, loaded it until it was chokkers and headed west. I met up with Carol at Gidgegannup WA where her parents lived.

CHAPTER SIX

MAGIC ELIXIR

When riches begin to come they
come so quickly, in such great
abundance, that one wonders where
they have been hiding during
all those lean years.
Napoleon Hill, Think And Grow Rich

We arrived in Western Australia straight after Christmas in time for the New Year. My first inclination was to not settle down straight away. Carol and I lived in a caravan during the cyclone period, so the weather did not settle down much either.

I decided to work for someone else for a change; so I got a job in Port Hedland as manager of a bakery. It was so bloody hot I used to drive to work in my undies with the air conditioner on full. But after 10 days I got back to wearing trousers because I quit: I was working for bloody crooks!

When I asked about ingredients the owner said: "A guy will call around in the evening. You tell him what you want and he'll bring it the following night."

The next night I got the supplies all right, but I noticed they had the name 'Poon Brothers' written all over them, and I thought: "Who's Poon Brothers? What the bloody hell's going on here?" Well, Poon Brothers were big caterers who were being robbed blind. This driver worked for Poon Brothers. He'd knock off all the stuff out of their store room and deliver it to me. That's what I had to bake with.

I didn't want to get involved with that so I walked out and said: "I don't want my pay...." I wouldn't work there for all the bloody money in the world.

I was too cranky. I needed to be my own boss. I realised I didn't enjoy working for anybody else. I also felt I'd 'gone backwards' after running my own show. I thought, 'bugger this' so I asked Carol if she knew of a bakery for sale in a town where there was an ocean and a river. She said that there was one in Augusta. It had two oceans, the Indian and the Southern Ocean, plus the Blackwood River – but they wanted a lot of money for the business.

At that time Augusta was really going ahead. A couple of years down the track, Margaret River became *the place* and Augusta hasn't changed much since. But Augusta put on a real spurt when we were there.

10,000 IN SUMMER

Carol and I drove to Augusta to check out the bakery. It was only a little town of about 500 people which explodes to about 10,000 in summer. That night we set up our tent in the caravan park and went uptown to get a feed of fish 'n' chips. We walked in, they gave us a ticket and we waited and waited for our number to come up. After waiting in a queue for half an hour they said, "Sorry, we've run out of food" and they shut up shop. We had to go to bed without a feed. All these holiday-makers were around but no one was really catering for them. I didn't like going to bed hungry.

The next morning the sun came up at 5 am so I got up starving and of course there was nothing open. In fact, there was no food available until the supermarket opened its doors at nine, and by that time I was famished. If anyone had been selling food in Augusta that day – they'd have had the early morning market all to themselves.

That morning I went to see the baker, Ken Whologan. He wanted $120,000 for the business, a lot of money. Already I could see the potential, I could feel it in my guts. So I said to Ken: "Yes, I'm pretty keen, I'd like to see how your bakery works...."

He said: "Can you come in and work tonight?"

I showed up that night but there was a dreadful row going on and by the morning his two bakers had walked off the job and they never came back – they had a problem with pay or something - so suddenly I was stuck there helping him because he had no one else to do the work. We wanted to buy his bakery, but I couldn't get out of the bloody place to organise my finances.

Although I'd 'sold' the Beechworth Bakery for $110,000, of which I had a half share, I didn't actually have the $55,000 cash because Johnny Gorkom's house hadn't sold; plus, I still owned the log cabin in Beechworth, which hadn't sold either. So getting the finance was a bit tricky for me. But the flour mills financed me and Ken kindly left some money in the business. It was no use trying the banks; Augusta didn't even have one. The bank manager would come to town on Fridays and handle everybody's business and I thought: "Shit, I could rob this bugger on his way out of town - especially in the tourist season." He would have been carrying a lot of money and I didn't exactly owe the banks any favours!

So I bought the business, but Ken Whologan pissed me off by telling everyone I would go broke and that he'd be right back. Another dream-taker! I don't like dream-takers and I felt I knew exactly what do to made it work. This was my third business.

I must admit it certainly wasn't easy. When I first went into the Augusta Bakery I was so broke and overcommitted, that we didn't even have enough money to feed ourselves. So I had to borrow $500 from my younger brother James and that was quite humiliating, but we were so sick of eating sandwiches that I wished I'd picked up that pay packet from those guys who were ripping off the Poons. Then things got much better – *fast*.

Where Ken used to make half a tray of apple cakes, I instantly did a whole tray. I'm very good at judging quantity. Twenty years ago, most bakeries in Australia would be empty by the end of lunchtime. I made sure I had plenty of product right up until closing time. Even today a lot of bakeries aren't worth going into after 2 pm. Ken's wasn't worth going in after 1 pm. So I instantly transformed the whole bloody business.

I know that you never sell the last four or five items on any tray. I know too that if you make a half a tray that's all you're gonna sell. I also know that if you make a full tray, you expect to sell a full tray – and you do. Furthermore, we started when the tourists were around, so I tripled Ken's figures in our first year.

WHITE ANTS

All through January we lived in an old 18-foot 50s-style caravan which was up on blocks. We then rented a small, old and dumpy house. I don't like renting houses and I wanted to buy my own place.

On the main drag there was an old four-bedroom house for sale. It was called 'Warmstone' and we liked it. Again I didn't get a bank loan. The vendor financed us.

We actually got ripped off bad because the house had been totally white-anted and the only thing holding the place together was the paint. Bloody hell, those white ants had eaten out the door jambs, the bearers, the studs and the noggins. You could stick your finger through the architraves if you pressed hard enough. When I wanted to get new wiring put in the electrician hopped in the roof and said, "Tom, the rafters are all gone. You can't put anything here." He also confirmed that there was not a white ant in the place, "There's nothing for them to eat, they've been and gone!" He had to run the conduit cable on the outside of the plaster.

A couple of years later, we wanted to buy a big two-storey brick house near Flinders Bay Beach, we needed to sell Warmstone, and a man called Colin Heath came to look at the house. He drove up in a big Mercedes Benz. I'm in business with this man today - with property in Busselton, Perth, Mandurah, Cairns and Denmark (I mean, Denmark, WA, of course). Compared to him, I'm a pretty small player, and our first meeting was disastrous.

COLIN HEATH

When Colin came to look at the property I told him all the bad things about the house. I was pretty honest; Carol and the real estate agent, Jim Challis, couldn't handle listen to me running the place down. They walked off.

I told Colin: "The roof leaks in the kitchen *but the bucket comes with the house*" and he thought I was a really funny bugger.

I told him the rafters in the ceiling were shot but that we had no white ants. I didn't tell him there was nothing left for the white ants to eat, but I told him the truth as far as I knew it. He ended up buying that house but before he did, he said: "Tom, I want a certificate that it's got no white ants."

He got that certificate but later on he rang me up and he said: "Bloody hell! There's no white ants but you didn't tell me there was hardly any timber left!"

When I was an apprentice in north-east Victoria, I always considered Frank Sinnett rich, because he had a nice home. But Colin Heath was probably the first really rich friend I had. In time, he pulled that house down, rebuilt it and turned it into a beautiful home. Virtually all he left standing was the big brick chimney in the middle of the house. I bought it for $35,000 and I'm pretty sure he spent in excess of $200,000 on it.

Over the years Colin has been a real mentor and friend. He taught me a lot about people. One night, we were in a restaurant in Perth where there were a lot of swanky types, and he turned to me and whispered: "Most of them aren't worth two-bob. They talk big, look flashy, but they're living on credit. Tom you could buy and sell most of them."

His wife, Faye, used to correct my grammar; she still does. She says: "Tom, don't say 'chimley' say 'chimney'. Don't say Eye-talian, it's Ee-talian, And don't swear all the time, it shows that you haven't got much of a vocabulary." Bloody hell.

He introduced me to some of his friends, and they all were rich too. Colin was proud to be my friend. He's very honest and very ethical. I waffle on and on, sometimes the dribble comes out both sides, Colin doesn't waste words; he's very direct. We've been friends now for nearly 30 years.

But he still gives me a hard time about the white ants.

DOLPHINS IN THE RIVER

With the sale of Warmstone, we bought the two-storey brick home overlooking Flinders Bay. The owner-builder left some money in it and I paid him off. Again vendor finance. I seemed to do that all the way along. I was beginning to have a thing about banks. They'd belittled my father all those years ago, and I still had a terrible phobia about anyone in authority.

I was always on the wrong side of the bloody desk.

We made it into a beautiful home. We had the cream bricks sand-rendered, we timber-lined it, we constructed a big central rock-faced fireplace and we put in a new kitchen using jarrah timber. We were very happy. A lot of good things happened in Western Australia. Carol was an incredible worker; we were a real

My fathers parents, James and Katy Toole, Ratoath, Co..Meath, Ireland.

L-R: Mum, Betty, Terry, Mickey and Dad (1949)
Dad always wore a tie, even when he was at work. And he always had a smoke hanging out of his mouth - even when it wasn't lit.

*Me in school uniform (1962).
I never learned to tie a tie
properly until I was in my 40s.*

*Our kitchen when we were
real young. We only had the
two rooms, the kitchen and
the bedroom.*

1971 - my first suit, the moustache came later.

The Beechworth Bakery when it was the Ideal Cafe, and when next door was still a clothes shop in 1974 when I first bought it in partnership with Betty and Allan.

Visiting my father's parents grave in Ratoath, Ireland.
Kate, Sharon and me.

Me in my comfort zone
with some of my team.
L-R: Kristen, me,
David, Marty and
Peter.

Happy family (1996)
L-R: (back) Me, Christine, (middle) Peter, (front) Kate, Matthew, Sharon.

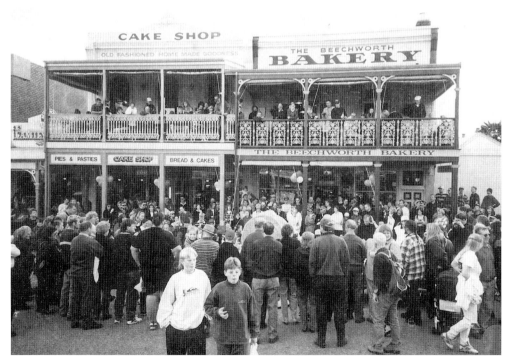

1998 Pie Eating Competition.

Our trusty A-model Ford. The Matchbox company created 20,000 replicas of this Beechworth Bakery vehicle. I drove this around Australia in 2001.

Staff group photo (1998).

Christine and I celebrating winning the 1998 Most Significant Regional Tourist Attraction of Victoria

Me with Jim who was my head baker in 1972. I went back with my family 27 years later and he is one of the main Elders of his tribe (1999).

We were young once... me and Christine.

Me, making dough.

The Bakery in the 1920s (dining rooms).

Out on the balcony of the Bakery with Christine's Dad, Steve, and my Mum, Nona.

'Serenity'. Me down on our river block.

In East Timor.

My sons, Peter and Matthew, were my two best taste testers back in the early days.

The family business. L-R: Me, Christine, our son Peter, granddaughter Adelaide, Adam (Sharon's husband), and my daughter Sharon.

Baking in East Timor.

A live baking demonstration in the shop with Dianne Forrest
and 'Sample Extraordinair' Keith McIntosh

'Works gotta be fun!' Me with some of my team on one of our Easter Parade Floats in Beechworth.

All dressed up for the 'Drive Back in Time' weekend festival in Beechworth.

Christine and myself with our business partners, Marty and Jo.

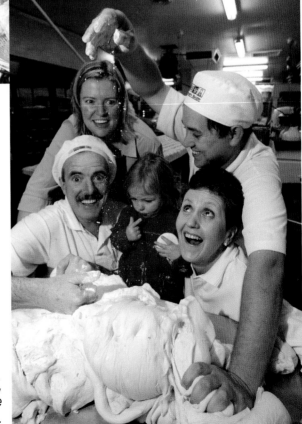

In the dough with myself, Sharon, Adam, Adelaide and Christine.

*Top & Bottom: Our Albury store - Who would have believed
we would have a bakery in a shopping centre!*

Getting into the festive season - the Echuca store decorated for Christmas.

Inside the Bendigo store.

team - it was very much a family business. It was purely a bakery and that was great - no lollies, no cigarettes, nothing like that.

The customers wanted it fresh and they wanted it now. We can sometimes lose the plot, we want to make the stuff now and sell it when we're ready. But I worked for the customer and I worked every hour I could. That bakery was very good to me. We made a lot of money in Augusta. I became quite famous. People still talk about my bakery.

I worked really hard in the holiday season when the tourists were around, then in the winter the locals would go up north and we enjoyed the quiet time. We had a little boat, the ocean was beautiful and there were dolphins in the river.

I must admit, I loved Augusta.

DAD, YOU'RE A BUSINESSMAN

Our bakery was a long walk from the main drag. There was a service station across the road as well as a fish 'n' chips shop, but there was a big gap between us and the centre of town, where the main businesses were – the newsagency, the pub, the butcher, the bottle shop and the Post Office.

People didn't just drift into our bakery; they had to make a real point of stopping. To encourage the customers to call in, I'd get my staff to park their cars in the street out the front so it looked like something was happening inside. As the shop started to get busy, we'd move our cars around the back. And then when it'd get quiet again in the afternoon, we'd move the cars back out the front. A crowd attracts a crowd.

Next, we bought a little Suzuki van which we filled with bread and cakes and we sold product to the people in swimming suits in the caravan park at Hamlin Bay. That's when I started to feel like I was working real hard and the caravan park owner had an easier life. Again, I did a fresh product and I kept it simple.

In a lot of ways I was before my time. I started to use fresh cream. Not many other bakers, if any, were using fresh cream in Western Australia. I also did a 'Tom's Special Loaf' which was cheese, bacon and onion. I became quite famous for that. I also did a Health Loaf.

The Catholic Church owned a block of land on the ocean side of the bakery. I was friendly with the priest and I ended up buying a small portion of that land, for which I designed a little eating area that I didn't build. It would have worked, but we ended up selling the business instead, so I gave the buyers the plan when I sold it. Twenty years later, and possibly by coincidence, the owners have built what looks like my original design.

I've never considered myself a businessman; I saw myself as 'just a baker'. Years later in Beechworth, my daughter Kate said to me: "Dad, you're a businessman, aren't you?" Until then, I'd never thought about it, but that's always what I wanted to be *a businessman!*

But I'm not a good businessman, I'm no great leader.

RACING BRAIN

I was a worrier though. I used to go to work every day with a football of fear in my guts and a can of worms in my head. I'd be thinking about next week, next month, just going, going, going – I had a racing brain, 'kangaroos in the back paddock' sorta thing.

I'd be worrying about all sorts of bloody things I shouldn't even be thinking about, like, "I hope the staff turns up for work". And when they did, I'd scream and carry on like a madman.

I don't know what I had to worry about as the bakery was doing real well. I was making heaps of money and I always thought I'd be happy if I had the material things. I hope I've grown up a bit since then.

I wrote to Dad one Father's Day and said: "Dad, if only I could be half as happy as you, then I would be a success." Today, I believe success is having peace of mind and being a good father and a good husband – which I never was. I don't know whether I am now. But being a good husband and a good father is the hardest job you'll ever have. Who wants to be a responsible father? I'd much rather go to work. It's a real escapism for me.

Speaking of escapism, along came the joints....

BLOWING JOINTS

I had a total of five employees. I employed Philip Ham and Dianne Forest. Years later when I bought back the Beechworth Bakery, they both came over to Victoria and Dianne is still with me today.

A couple of the others were well-educated guys who had been to uni and who were into drugs. They would smoke joints at morning tea break. Mick would say: "Tom, you need to relax. Toke on this."

"What do you mean Toc?"

"Not Toc ... toke!"

I didn't care what anyone did so long as they did their work. I'd put up with their behaviour as long as they put up with mine. Even though I didn't smoke grass, I used to get invited to lots of drug parties. When it came to party invitations, I was accepted by all sorts of social groups, just like in Maningrida. To me, the doctor's parties were the same as the hippie parties.

I suppose that's one of my strengths. If people have got ear studs, a nose studs, tatts, pony tails, nipple rings or whether they're blowing smoke rings – who am I to judge them?

I didn't need the marijuana. Alcohol had become the drug of my choice.

MAGIC ELIXIR

Although I occasionally had a social drink, I never really drank much before I got to Western Australia. Until then I could take it or leave it, but that had now changed.

I remember quite clearly saying to my wife, "I *need* a drink". I'd crossed that invisible line, I didn't want a drink, I *needed* one!

Because I was a shift worker and I slept during the day, and again in the evening, alcohol seemed to help me sleep. I also found that if I had a drink I could talk to people. For the first time in my life I felt comfortable around people if I had a drink in me. *Wow!* It was what I'd been looking for all my life – this magic elixir. Wonderful stuff! Better than mother's milk! It changed my life (did it ever!).

I used to come home from work and have a drink, then I'd have another until I got it down to my fingertips. I'd have a couple more, get it down to my toes, and I loved it. I'd feel good all over and then I'd go to bed. I drank for the effect – but that's another sadder story.

EVERYBODY ELSE'S PADDOCK

Our marriage started to go bad in Augusta. We thought the problem was 'being in business' because we were both working really hard and Carol and I looked longingly at all these holiday-makers having great times on the beach. But it wasn't the business; the problem was me. I wasn't happy. Here I was at 30 thinking that everybody else's job looked easier. I know every business has its drawbacks; nevertheless, to me, the grass always seemed greener on the other side

Baking is a hard game because it's labour-intensive and I didn't even know whether I still wanted to stay in it. I fantasised about being a caravan park owner – where people in swimsuits would just wander in, hand over lots of money and park their vans.

Everybody else's paddock looked greener. I know today to be careful for where the grass is greener is often where the sewerage comes out.

MAURITIUS

Carol stopped talking to me and our marriage was fast going bad. I was scared I was going to lose her and I told that to one of my bakers. Trevor's marriage counselling advice was, "Tom take her to Mauritius – it's a wonderful place."

So I rang up the travel agent who said: "Tom you can't get to Mauritius that easy. There's only one flight a week but you're in luck, there's a cancellation, so there's two seats available tomorrow." I decided to grab them. *Don't wait until you're bloody organised!*

As Carol and I were flying out the next day, I had to get everything sorted out really quickly for the trip. First of all I had to find Mick my baker to tell him to hold the fort while I was gone, but when I found him Mick was shitfaced. He'd OD-ed on some bloody drugs, so I pinned a note on his shirt explaining that he had to look after the place while I was gone.

During the seven-hour flight, Carol and I talked about business, marriage, and where we were heading with our lives. Sometimes you've just got to do that with your partner.

When we got to Mauritius at night time, lots of people were standing around with guns at the Port Louis Airport. They gave us a bit of a fright when they took away our passports but they returned them once we had booked our accommodation. In the cab we got another scare when the driver started filling it up with his mates. We thought, "Shit, this is scary" but they were okay – they didn't rob us.

We ended up in a beautiful chalet and Carol and I fell madly in love for the night. The next day we hired push bikes and went off on a discovery adventure exploring the island. However, at the end of the day we pulled into a local shop where I saw cheap rotgut rum for

$1 a bottle. So I bought the rum, which was rough – but it was great. So it wasn't long before I was in trouble in Mauritius.

We enjoyed ourselves heaps for the first week and then the fears came back and I decided it was time to go home. However, we had to stay for another two weeks because we couldn't get a flight out of the bloody place. I rang up my little daughter Sharon in tears on the radio-telephone telling her that I was missing her – and if you've ever talked on a radio-telephone, you'll know that your voice echoes - so this teary mad crying person was coming back at me — and it was my own bloody self!

We were stuck there for three weeks and still the marriage was no better. Not long after we were home, Carol announced that she was pregnant with Kate and I announced I wanted to sell the bakery. Sharon and Kate were breast fed in the bakery, they were little bakery kids.

SELLING THE BUSINESS

I wanted $250,000 for the bakery when $250,000 was a lot of dough.

John Noonan wanted to buy it and I didn't take to John too well. He was an educated man from a fairly rich family - and I resented him because he wore a bloody calculator watch.

I was teaching him for a month before he was to take over the business and I was giving of my best. I'd tell him good things, which he would have found useful if only he'd bloody-well pay attention. I'd say, "This is how we do this" and he'd push the buttons on his watch. I put up with this nonsense for a time and then one night, I said: "This is how we make our pastry." John had a bit of a glance, shrugged his shoulders and just walked off. He wasn't interested.

Well, I lost it. I really lost it! I grabbed John around the neck and tried to stick him in the oven and he was a heavy guy – bigger than me.

Philip Ham, my apprentice, didn't know what to do. He could see I was trying to kill the bastard. He knew not to say, "Hey Tom, let him go" because if he'd said that I was liable to grab Philip around the bloody neck too! Phil tapped me on the shoulder gently instead and said, "Tom, are these scones cooked yet?" and it sorta broke the madness and I let go of John.

At home I said to Carol: "I don't think John's going to buy the bakery."

She said: "Why not?"

I said: "I just tried to stick him in the oven.... I'm sorry."

But John was sillier than me. He turned up at midnight the next night to start work again, and he ended up buying the business. I probably didn't want him to buy it; I loved the Augusta bakery, it was my baby.

MY IRELAND HOME

After we sold the business we were cashed-up, (we were pretty cashed-up anyway) so we headed off to Europe for two months. We left our daughters with Carol's mother and I missed them something terrible. Sharon was three and Kate was one year old.

Carol and I travelled throughout Europe and we had some great times. We went to a big Bakery Expo in Germany. We also went to Czechoslovakia, East Berlin and other Communist countries. We went to the Greek Isles, Holland, Austria, lots of other countries, and that trip was the first time I went to Ireland and I looked up my relatives.

I remember one night when my Irish folks were gathered together, my second cousin Jim Collins said: "Tom, do you want a drink of poteen?"

I said: "What's that?"

He said: "It's alcohol."

No one else wanted to drink it, so I said: "Yes, I'll give it a try." I took a mouthful and I couldn't bloody breathe! Hell! It was like drinking petrol. It was incredibly good stuff; I loved it. It helped me mix in and I felt very comfortable. It was made from distilled potato.

Jim said: "Tom, how about taking a couple of bottles back for your father?"

I said: "How do I get it through customs?"

"Just tell them it's Holy Water," which wasn't entirely untrue.

I got it through customs, but Dad never got it. I gradually drank the bloody lot.

Dad had never kept contact with his Irish relations. They thought he was dead. Before we went to Ireland, Dad wrote me a long letter with pages and pages describing his childhood haunts and the names of the people he used to mix with. I ended up meeting lots of them and I checked out where he grew up. My Dad was a real story-teller and I remembered his stories when I saw all these castles, abbeys and churches that I'd heard about all through my childhood. Visiting Ireland was the highlight of my trip. I felt at home.

In Europe, Carol and I had lots of spending money which was quite exciting because she never grew up with money; neither did I, yet here we were living it right up!

Two months of partying in Europe didn't help our marriage at all.

SELLING THE HOUSE

When we came home, our first job was to sell our house.

It was one of the bigger homes in the little town, and we wanted about $120,000, which was a lot of money. I didn't have a good opinion of the real estate agent because he'd tried to pressure me into buying the block of land next to the bakery on the Perth side. I hadn't seen him for bloody years, and now here he was selling my house. His sister and his brother-in-law wanted to buy it.

I was sitting around the dining room table with the three of them. I'd had a couple of drinks before they arrived, I said to them, "Let's have a drink" so I pulled my flagon out and I signed the papers. Then I started to relax, thinking they'd signed too. We all got talking and next minute I started telling the real estate agent what I really thought of him. I explained his pedigree in full. Oh God, I fired up. Geez I was in top gear! Next minute, the couple got up and left. And so I said to the real estate agent, who I'd just been bagging horrifically: "What's up with them?"

He stood up, walked to the door and said, "I'll find out" and they all hopped in the car and left immediately.

That was an expensive drink. I had to drop my price by 10 grand plus I had to apologise, which was just about as bad as losing the money. I also said I'd throw in all the furniture for good measure; plus, I said I'd do this, that and the other. They had us by the short and curlies because we were ready to head off around Australia, and I didn't want to be stuck with this expensive house any longer.

LEAVING WA

When we left Augusta, Kate was just two years old. We'd had an amazing lifestyle and we left knowing that we'd had a great business in a wonderful town. We made lots of money and I could have lived there happily ever after. But I wasn't happy inside of myself and neither was Carol – we were both running; the marriage wasn't real good. We blamed the business; we believed we were working too hard, so I promised Carol that I wouldn't go back into business.

We bought a Land Cruiser and a 23 foot three-room caravan and headed off around Australia. We left Western Australia via Albany, Esperance, Kalgoorlie and at one time we looked at settling in the Barossa Valley, South Australia. We travelled throughout that State and ended up back in Tocumwal for Christmas 1983. After a few months of travelling I started to get bored.

I went to Beechworth to visit Betty and Allan. I'd been away from Beechworth for six-and-a-half years, and on this visit I saw the town with fresh eyes. During the years I'd been away I had also travelled to Malaysia, Indonesia, Norfolk Island (I went over there to look at buying a bakery) and significantly, I'd been to Europe where I saw the full potential of tourism.

I went back to Beechworth with a head full of ideas, and although the condition of the bakery saddened me a bit, it also offered a whole lot of opportunities.

CHAPTER SEVEN

HONEST WITH TOM

To love oneself is the beginning
of a lifelong romance.
Oscar Wilde

When I was in Western Australia Dad often used to say to me: "Tom, I'm praying for you."

"Why is that silly old bugger praying for me?" I thought: "I've got money – look at me, I'm doing all right. I've got the big two-storey house, I've got all the material stuff, and he's saying he's praying for me?" But he could see that I wasn't happy. Alcohol had become a big problem in my life and work was consuming me.

Years later I went back and admitted: "I know what the problem is Dad...."

He had tears running down his face; they were tears of happiness, and he said: "Thank God! I've been praying for you for years."

My Dad died in 1988. He lived to see my daughters Sharon and Kate, as well as Peter, my first son. He died when he was one month short of turning 80. I managed to spend a fair bit of time with Dad before he died.

In a way I was quite relieved to see Dad go because he was in a lot of pain for many years. I didn't grieve a lot. Dad was proud, he didn't like being put in a wheelchair – especially the way Mum pushed it.

When I was in Western Australia I was pretty sure Dad was going to die and that I would never see him again; I used to cry about it. So I shouted him and Mum a trip to Augusta and I hired a wheelchair for him.

On that visit, I remember upsetting Mum. I made her so mad that she stormed out of our house, pushing Dad down the road leading out of town. Here we were, on the most south-west tip of Australia and Mum was threatening to push him across the Nullarbor Plain in a wheelchair all the way back to Victoria. Geez, she could have got into the Guinness Book of Records!

KNOCKED OUT COLD

When I went back to Beechworth I immediately saw that no one had really tapped into its tourism potential.

Instead, I saw an Ideal Bakery that was far from ideal. It was bankrupt and finished. It was falling down, mouse infested, rat infested and it even had a possum living in the bakehouse. Even worse, the possum was friendly and it's very hard to get rid of a possum once it gets friendly. We'd take it into the bush, and two days later the bloody thing was back.

You'd come to work in the morning and it'd be sitting on the bench eating the pastie vegetables. It finally disappeared when a restaurant opened up down the road. We never saw it ever again, thank God.

I wanted to buy the business back but Johnny Gorkom wouldn't sell because he was in such financial straits. He was also a mess mentally, even physically – which is sad considering that he was a former boxing champion. Nobody in the state could beat him in the ring, but he wasn't winning a round in the bakery.

Johnny was finished. The Council was going to slap a health order on the premises but he still wouldn't sell. He couldn't. He didn't know how.

So I bought the clothes shop next door, then I went to see him and said: "Johnny, if you don't sell to me, I'm going to open up next door."

He replied: "Tom, I can't sell. I don't know what to do. I've got no other place to live" (he was living above the bakery).

I said: "Johnny, why don't you head off around Australia?"

And he said: "Can I have your caravan?" I said okay. Then the bastard also wanted my Land Cruiser!

I said: "Buy your own bloody car!"

Finally, I had to pay him $110,000 for a business that was bankrupt. Johnny also took my caravan as part of the deal. The day we bought it we got in a front-end loader, a truck and a team of men who chucked out the benches plus all the broken machinery. We also shovelled up the mouse shit, got rid of the dead birds and the dead mice and we cleaned up the whole place. (In time we bulldozed and rebuilt the whole bakehouse and while all that was going on we baked in the shop next door until we rebuilt.)

I'd forgotten that it was such a maze! There were five different floor levels; it was shocking. Nearly everything had to be pulled down, fixed or reconstructed. I wanted a decent bakery.

Betty and Allan came in again as partners and a lot of the people who formerly worked for me came back. Previously, I never drank, but this time I was drinking. So I was a bit of a different person to work for.

I yelled and screamed even louder.

END OF MARRIAGE

Back home, things weren't going well between me and Carol. Being a workaholic is a respectable addiction, but in reality it can be a form of escapism. While at work I was in my comfort zone and having the perpetual excuse of working meant I could avoid facing up to my responsibilities of being a good father and husband – and that was just one of the problems.

I wanted to go to a marriage counsellor, but Carol was so pissed off that she wouldn't even talk to me – let alone a counsellor.

I owned a gun, so one day I got it down, loaded it, put it in my mouth and tried it out for size. If you've ever put a loaded gun in your mouth, they taste very cold and oily – they're nothing like a sausage roll.

But I didn't pull the trigger because my thinking was all out of whack and I realised I didn't want to shoot myself with an unregistered gun. That's how silly I was. So I got Carol to come with me to the police station. We registered the gun so I could kill myself, but the next day she was gone. I think she thought I was going to shoot her.

After being in the business for six months Carol left me for keeps. And when she left I fell madly in love with her. Funny that, we often do the same with staff and suppliers – we don't appreciate what we've got until we lose them.

I had taken little Kate out for a bike ride and when I came home there was a "Dear Tom" letter on the bed. It said something like: "I've gone, don't follow me....". I have two wonderful daughters and luckily Carol left the kids with me because without them I probably would have necked myself. When Carol left, Kate was just three and Sharon was five. Kate and Sharon gave me strength, but I still couldn't be grateful; I felt sorry for myself. I was devastated; I was a total, total, total demolition job. I felt a failure. I couldn't go to work. I couldn't face anybody. I wanted to die.

Hell, I was a mess, I was falling apart like a Chinese motorbike. I went back to the solicitor – the same guy who advised me not to pinch Carol's frying pan – and said: "Graham, I need help!"

He said: "I can see that." And he reached for the phone.

I said, "What are you doing?"

He said, "I'm ringing the mental home!"

I said: "No, you don't understand! My wife, she's got the credit cards!"

"That's the least of your worries," he said. Then he tried to calm me down, and suggested that I go to the mental home for a rest. I said 'no way'. I wouldn't go to the mental home because I remembered the song, "*They're coming to take me away, ha ha he he ho ho*" it used to play it in my head all the bloody time. *Ha ha he he ho ho*. Graham got me to a lifeline counsellor in Albury. He said, "Tell and get well".

There was no way I was going up the hill to the bloody mental home - even though I always thought I was going to end up there one day.

So it was bye, bye Carol, my business partner, my bookkeeper and the mother of my two girls.

DYSFUNCTIONAL

The break-up was mainly my fault. I always used to put all my shit onto Carol, telling her how useless she was - and if you tell someone often enough they'll believe you. We can do that with our staff too. I used to tell Carol she was a hopeless mother and wife – but that was all my shit, I was talking to myself. I was the hopeless parent – so ironically, she left me with the kids. She wanted to keep partying.

She also left because I had become a workaholic and I wasn't much fun to live with. I'd sleep in the day and work through the night, I was an anti-social bugger; it suited me down to the ground.

At that time I had no balance in my life. I didn't know how to let go. But when Carol left it was the best thing that happened to me – I didn't think so at the time but I needed to learn to be grateful. *In every disaster lies an opportunity.* And boy, what a disaster!

I'm not the greatest father; I'm never going to win the Father of the Year award, but mind you, if Bob Hawke could – bloody hell, there's hope for me yet!

So Carol left me and went to Fiji. She met somebody else within two days. When she rang me, I said: "Where are you?"

She said: "I'm in Fiji, don't follow me."

I said: "Have you met somebody?"

She said: "Yes."

I said: "Are you in love?"

She said: "I think so."

Well, both of us knew lots about lust – not a lot about love.

Before Carol left, I worked hard in the bakery. But when she left I couldn't show my face at work or around town. I was too devastated to face my staff. I couldn't go back into the business because it was such a big part of our marriage and revisiting those memories hurt too much. I couldn't look at the spot where I first popped my head up and asked Carol, "Are you married or not?"

Her answer was "sort of…" and I didn't know what she meant at the time. Now I knew exactly what she meant.

ONE-MINUTE WONDER

When Carol left, it was my personal rock bottom. You wouldn't believe the self-pity! I was so low that Jenny, my counsellor, phoned the mental home and told them "hold that room" because she was convinced I'd be coming in. Yes, *my wife had actually left me* and I never thought it would happen. I didn't get married to end up with my wife leaving. That just wasn't part of my make-up.

Without Carol, I had difficulty doing simple day-to-day duties. She did all the bookwork. I didn't even have the ability to write a cheque. It's pretty incredible - here I was into my fourth business and I couldn't write out cheques because I had no confidence in my spelling. I can spell much better today, but in those days – I could hardly spell at all. I would have had a hard time spelling 'a thousand' or any number like that.

I got so low, I didn't even want to get out of bed.

I got so low, I couldn't face anyone.

I felt as if I was the only person in the world who had experienced a break-up.

Without my kids, this story might not have had a happy ending. But Sharon and Kate needed me, and that was about the only thing that kept me going. I don't think I was the only one who was thinking, 'Tom's lost the plot'. I think a lot of people around town were thinking that.

When you get that low, the only place you can go is up (or six feet under). I had to start 'going up' and going out was a good start. So I had to start facing people, I had to start acting like a responsible single parent. I had to go to the school, I even had to go to the supermarket.

I used to think, "Everyone's talking about me" but I was just a flash in the pan. The reality is, when your wife leaves you're a one-minute wonder. Most people are only worried about themselves; they weren't concerned with 'Tom's marriage break-up'. They were all too busy talking about their own lives. Of course, they like to gossip for a little while, but something else quickly comes into the picture. However, I was hiding away in my house, because I thought everyone was talking about me.

GOING NUTS

I was totally devastated. I had become pretty dysfunctional in lots of areas of my life. One of the many reasons I resented Carol leaving was that I couldn't even put film in the camera. There's a big 12-month gap in my photo album until I learned how to insert film. I didn't know how to load the Minolta, so I couldn't take any more photos. Little things like that bugged me. *Little things are the only things.*

I hit the lowest of the low. I used to cry myself to sleep. I felt sad for my children; oh God I was low! Sometimes I'd get very angry; I was very suicidal – homicidal, at times. It took a long time for me to climb out of that. With the help of my counsellor and the 12-step program that I had joined I finally scrambled out of that big, dark hole.

My life had become totally unmanageable and I was stuffing up bad. The business really suffered because I wasn't in it, nor was Carol. Instead, I was staying home trying to figure how to be a responsible single parent, as well as trying to work out how the washing machine worked, and the dishwasher, the dryer and the bloody oven.

When I first went to see Jenny I kept telling her: "I'm mad, I should be seeing a psychiatrist not a counsellor!"

There was all this crazy stuff rolling around in my head from my childhood (in fact, all through my life) that I haven't written about. There was this driving insanity that was building up inside my head, and there seemed no way of releasing it. For many months I blamed everybody else for my problems, and that seemed to help.

HONEST WITH TOM

In every disaster lies an opportunity. The break-up made me stop for long enough to take a look in the mirror. Without that, I would have simply kept racing through my life blaming everybody else because I found it much easier to pass the buck. I'd think, "If them bastards would only get their act together, if only Philip would do this right, and if only Margaret would do that, everything would be okay". But nowadays I have learned that *if it's to be, it's up to me.*

It's not up to my mother, it's not up to my wife, it's not up to my kids, if it's to be – it's up to me. What a simple philosophy that is.

This counsellor had walked me through my childhood, she had listened to me blame the school, the nuns, my mother ... but when I got through the list, I ran out of excuses, so I rang her up and cancelled my next appointment because I thought: "I've run out of people to blame. I've got nothing else to say. So what's the sense in going?" But I showed up anyway.

Jenny said: "Tom, you've got to get honest."

I said: "I'll go broke!"

She said: "No, you've got to get honest with **YOU**". She meant that I had to stop blaming everybody else for my problems. I had to start taking responsibility for my state of mind. I tried everything else and that hadn't worked, so I decided to follow her advice and I slowly got my life back in order. Just because I hit rock bottom didn't instantly mean that I got my act together. I stopped screaming at employees for a while, but then I got back into that habit because that was all I knew about management. It took a long time to change that. I was probably sillier and crazier in the first two years after joining the 12-step program than I was before, so it took me a long time to straighten up Tom O'Toole.

However, with a lot of help, one of the by-products of me getting my head back together was that I gave away the grog. Today, I don't drink at all. I haven't had a drink for well over 20 years.

DYE-BOMBING THE STAFF

In the meantime, my business was in real trouble. My brother-in-law Allan was a partner for about four years until I bought him out. I also had another partner from Western Australia, my former apprentice Philip Ham. For a while Allan and Philip were running the business, I must admit they weren't running it too well, but they were getting no help from me.

Allan, whom I thought was pretty good with figures, in fact wasn't. It came as a bit of a shock when one day the bank manager rang me up at home and said, "Tom, are you going to put some money in the account?" (There was a $20,000 interest payment due.)

I rang Allan and said: "The bank wants some money for an interest payment."

He said: "There should be plenty in the account."

The bank manager said, "There's none!"

Allan didn't believe him and shrugged it off. He said: "It should be fine."

Well, there was bloody nothing. We'd been robbed!

So we rang the police. The detectives came in and found the security leak. Allan was doing up all the money, putting the bag down before going to the bank and somebody was pinching money straight out of the bag. By the time he'd gone to the bank, they'd already helped themselves. I don't know how many people had their hand in the bag but we only caught one.

So the detectives put a dye-bomb in the money bag. I said, "bugger this" and left; it was all too much for me, because I trusted all my employees. I had about 23 at the time, because that was as many as I could yell at. I was already going through all these difficult emotions; now I had to add suspicion to the list.

I came back later that day and the money had been pinched again. I said to Allan: "Have they caught them yet?" Allan said: "No, they thought it was this one, then they thought it was that one."

The dye-bomb had certainly gone off, dye was bloody everywhere. Whoever pinched the money had it all over their hands, so they had to get a look at everybody's hands. At first they thought it was a baker. Then they were pretty sure it was the lady doing the dishes because she'd sink her hands into the water every time they went near her. This went on for maybe an hour. But it wasn't her.

Then they thought it was the lady next door in the video shop; she was renting the premises from us. She had a bit of a criminal record, so the detectives said: "It must be her because she has access to the back of the bakery." Plus, she wasn't showing her hands. But it wasn't her either. This just went on and on and on.

Finally, they interviewed every staff member and about at 10.00 pm they found it was a cake decorator, a girl who lived in Wodonga. She admitted to pinching $7000 and the police said: "Tom, I'd hate to imagine what was really pinched if she admitted to that!" Probably other people were having a field day too.

She was pinching the money for her boyfriend, not for herself. In the end she moved to Adelaide and paid the $7000 back.

I got a counsellor to help her and she wrote me a really nice letter some months later and again in 2002 after reading this book.

SINGLE PARENT

It was time for me to face the real world; so it was a real learning curve for me. I had to do all these things like going into supermarkets, which I'd never done before. I also had to buy clothes for Sharon and Kate. I had no idea of colour coordination but I knew if I bought one-colour track suits, instead of skirts and tops, I wouldn't have to worry about what went with what. I wasn't at all house-trained. I didn't even know how to do the dishes. My Mum wasn't great at doing dishes either.

Keith McIntosh stood by me. Keith and his wife Joan had brought up five kids and they were very happily married. Keith would come out to my place. He would never lecture me. We washed the dishes together and he taught me how to put the clothes through the dryer, and here he was – working as a psych nurse with his own family to look after, but he always found time for his mate Tom. He didn't know what to do to heal my state of mind; he didn't have a bloody clue how to heal my hurt, he was just there for me. My family, weren't there for me, they had their own paddocks to mow – which is pretty normal.

I thought I loved my first wife, but really it wasn't a love it was a need. I needed my wife. I don't know about loving her – I didn't know what love was. I needed her to run my business, to hold my hand, to do the washing. When my wife left I ruined so many of the kids' clothes. I'd put them in the wash, they'd shrink, and then I'd put them in the drier and they'd get smaller – they were good for doll's clothes. Furthermore, I could only cook in a bakehouse; put me in a domestic kitchen, and I couldn't cook for nuts. I'd cook sausages, beans and potatoes.

Some other people were good to me. Rose, who cleaned my house, and her husband Noel gave me wonderful support. Noel understood what I was going through as he'd gone through a marriage break-up himself. It happens! It happens to a lot of people even though I felt I was the only one who'd ever gone through it. During this period I met other people who'd had the same difficulties. Oh God, it was a low time. The kids would get sick, they'd wet the bed all the time. "Dad!" they'd cry in the night, "Dad! Dad!" It wasn't much fun.

Meanwhile, Carol would phone from Fiji and I could hear all these parties - the music and the laughter in the background. *Oh God almighty!*

OH CAROL!

Then Carol wrote telling me she wanted to have a baby to this Fijian guy. Well, I was devastated because I was madly in love with her. I was too much of a mess to keep my own company; I would have turned a pity party into a wake, so I visited friends who had a coffee shop where the Bank Restaurant is today. They were flat out with a shopful of people all wanting service, so they said to me: "What does your counsellor do when you're in this state?"

I said: "She makes me lay down on the floor and take deep breaths."

They said: "For chrissakes do that."

And there they were stepping over me while cooking the dinners. By the time they'd got rid of the customers (I think I helped get rid of them) they took me aside and said: "Tom, you only have today. Just one day at a time, that's all you've got. It takes nine months to make a baby – *nine whole months*."

Aggh! Carol's baby! Off I went again – although I eventually settled down and understood what they were trying to say.

And today, I know that's all I've got. Any one can get through one day, even when they get bad news. It's only when you join those two awful eternities together - yesterday and tomorrow - that you go mad.

Carol didn't end up having that baby so I frightened off all those customers for nothing.

She ended up leaving that Fijian bloke and getting re-married in Australia.

I AM A GOOD BAKER

Because a lot of areas of my life were becoming even more unmanageable, I did a course in basic communication and self-awareness with Lifeline. (Lifeline is a great Australia-wide organisation. I'm still involved with Lifeline today.) This brought me to a realisation that I had little awareness of anyone else's feelings and emotions and that I was very bloody selfish and self-centred. As a result of the Lifeline Self-Awareness and Basic Communication course I decided to stop hiding away and I started to meet people. Things started to change dramatically in lots of ways. I started getting honest with myself

My wife leaving me was the best thing that ever happened to me because I had to look at *me* and think: "What do I want out of life? Where do I want to be? What do I want to do? Do I want to be a baker? Or do I want to run a caravan park?" I had to ask myself the big questions and face the big answers.

I had lots of self-doubts and a very low self-worth, especially without my wife. I didn't even know if I was a 'good' baker or a 'good' businessman.

About four months after Carol left I went back to Western Australia. I took the kids to visit their grandmother who had moved to Augusta.

Ben Tas, a friend of mine who had a bakery in Busselton, wanted me to help him bake one night. He was having a few problems with his doughs and he needed some advice. I was out of the baking game at the time; I'd been out since my wife left. I felt a failure even as a baker.

Ben wouldn't take no for an answer and so I helped him do his baking. I could see his problem straight away, so I started giving him advice which he followed, and then he said to me: "Shit! That was so simple, why didn't I think of that?" He kept praising me up all night, saying all this affirmative stuff. The words I remember most are: "Geez Tom, you're a bloody good baker."

I used to judge myself and I would conclude that I'm not a good baker - and today I still tell people that I'm no good.

But whatever I say, deep down I know that *I am a good baker,* and it all started with Ben.

THE SUN COMES UP

I left him early that morning feeling pretty good about myself. I got in the car and drove back to Augusta. For years I'd seen the spectacular West Australian sunrises and here it was again – the sun rising out of the ocean, a big ball of golden light brightening up the whole world.

And as the rays of the sunshine started hitting me I felt, "God never made a nothing".

In my past, I always felt I was a nothing, but if "God never made a nothing" then I must be a something!

Therefore, I couldn't possibly be a useless, hopeless, worthless, dickhead, shovel. I wasn't a 'justa'.

Not 'just a' baker – but a BAKER, and there's a very big difference.

Despite the separation, Carol and I didn't become enemies. She was in Queensland somewhere with her Fijian boyfriend, when she rang me. I told her I had been helping Ben and that Ben kept telling me how good a baker I was.

"Of course you're a bloody good baker!" she said. But I didn't *know* I was a good baker – no one had ever really told me. And so my self-image was gradually beginning to change.

TURNING BEECHWORTH AROUND

In 1984, Beechworth wasn't much of a town; there were lots of empty shops, with quite a few boarded up. Today I get credited a lot for turning Beechworth around, but I was just there at the right time. Plus I had a bit of money so I could afford to pull down and re-build the bakery. I also advertised on regional TV and I invited people to visit Beechworth.

When I came to town the people said: "Tom, everyone shops in Albury and Wang!"

I said: "Well, I'm going to invite them to come to here." And that's all I do – I just invite them to come to Beechworth. It's so simple, but it's not easy.

We use the slogan 'Australia's Greatest Bakery'. We tell them we're famous. And if you tell them often enough they'll believe you. As far as we know we have the highest sales for any stand-alone retail bakery in Australia. There may be others who are taking more – but the Taxation Department doesn't know about them. Other bakeries also do wholesale and discounting, whereas we are totally cash. I like cash.

If anyone wants a 20 per cent discount, I want to cut out 20 per cent of the ingredients, and it doesn't taste real good.

AND IT WAS CHRISTINE ... WOW!

I was in the bakehouse one day when Keith called out to me. I followed him outside and there, sitting in a car, was the brown-haired girl I last saw when I was 24. Keith said, "Do you remember this girl, Tom?"

And it was Christine. Wow.

I hadn't seen Christine since we'd broken up. She had been a nurse in Melbourne. I hadn't seen Christine for many years – and here she was. I looked at her and remembered how much I'd hurt this girl, and thought: "She wasn't the problem, I was." I went back home, rang up my counsellor immediately and made another booking.

I said, "I'd like to see you," and she said, "Let's catch up over a drink"

I said: "I don't drink any more. Come out for a coffee instead." She came out for a coffee and I thought – wow, this is wonderful! But she then told me that she was off to London in two days' time. Bloody hell!

However, it was really good not to rush into another relationship, Christine didn't cloud the issue of the Carol break-up and I was still an emotional mess. I wrote to Christine a bit, and I wrote Carol heaps of love letters plus lots of crazy stuff. In time, I ended up visiting Christine in London. We went to Portugal for a holiday where we had the time of our lives. We were two totally different people from when we first met, and from when I gave her that big pasho at her back door all those years ago.

And then I came home while Christine stayed in London working. In time, she travelled around Europe and America, while I was getting my life back together in Beechworth. This all happened in 1984-85.

SELF HELP

It took a long time for me to let go of Carol and to get on with life. Christine gave me the time to work my way through all my problems while Jenny my counsellor said: "Tom, stop being so focused on your wife, start focusing on *you*. If you get better, everything else around you will get better." So then I had to start on the biggest investment of my life, I started to invest in me.

I was at home by myself heaps, so I started to read. I spent a lot of time reading good stuff – books on self-help and self-awareness. I thought Norman Vincent Peale was one of the greatest writers, although when I recently re-read *The Power Of Positive Thinking* I was astonished at how religious it was. I wasn't too much into religion. I used to pray but I never went to church.

I sat under a tree for a week at Merimbula and read *Work Smarter Not Harder* by Michael le Boeuf and Jack Collis and it also helped me change. It really helped me get focused on my business. I also went to a couple of seminars by Winston Marsh and Lisa Jane McGuiness in Melbourne and I thought wow! I'd never been to a seminar before.

That whole self-help stuff really did turn my head around. One of the early books that also helped me a lot was Bob Ansett's autobiography. He did a lot of things with Budget that were revolutionary in his day. I also enjoyed *Think And Grow Rich* by Napoleon Hill, plus a couple of Tom Peters' books. I sent the best ones to Carol who was still in Fiji. I wanted to save her too. That was the end of my books.

I started to read psychology books about human emotions and I started trying to get an awareness of other people's feelings. I tried to control my yelling and I tried to stop ruling by fear. I stopped being a seagull manager. I guess you could say, I changed. It wasn't easy, it just didn't happen overnight and I struggle with some of these things even today.

I bought state-of-the-art equipment for the bakehouse, so we no longer needed to work all night like we did in Augusta, which is no good for anybody's marriage.

The first 12-18 months after Carol left were very foggy, I can't remember much and I don't think I want to remember those days – but after a few more dramas, I was on the way up. I wrote my goals on paper so I knew what I was aiming for. I sketched what I wanted my bakery to become and then I started building it.

I was the world's greatest worrier. One day I heard someone say that *he* was the world's greatest worrier, and I remember instantly saying: "Well, he can be – I don't want to be." Like I said, I used to go to work every day with a football of fear in my guts and a can of worms in my head, and then I learned that I just had to get through *now*. By that I mean that I don't 'project'. I used to project into the future or else I'd be living in the past. Today, I just try to live in the now. I learned that you can be as happy as you make up your mind to be. And I learned I only have today, I only have now.

I certainly plan for the future: today I plan the future a lot. But I don't project, I don't live there. If I'm going on holidays to America I don't say: "Geez I'm going to have a great time, I'll be doing this, I'll be doing that…". That's the kind of projection I avoid, because it's worthless. Yes, I plan my future, but I don't live there; like I planned this bakery but I don't live there either.

I did a lot of self-analysis because I realised I didn't really know who Tom O'Toole was. I had to do a lot of thinking and I even had to ask myself: "Do I want to be justa baker?" One day I made the commitment. I looked around and thought: "I'm gonna be a BAKER."

Not 'justa' baker – there is no such word as 'justa'.

I decided to be a real baker, boots 'n all.

BE GRATEFUL

I used to love having pity parties all by my lonesome. One day I was working in the bakery crying, "Poor me, poor me - pour me…a drink". I was feeling real sorry for myself when one of my employees, Jeanette, came around the corner, spotted me and said: "You look awful. What the heck's bothering you Tom?"

"Poor me," I said. "Here I am at 32 and I've just woken up to myself; I've wasted all these years being a bloody seagull manager and an arsehole."

She said: "What have you got to cry about? You're lucky that you woke up to yourself. My Dad's never going to wake up to himself. He's never gonna get a life, he's gonna die a drunken, lonely old man."

And that's it, you've got to be grateful. And today I am grateful. That's one of my secrets of personal happiness.

> I hear people saying:
> "I'm having a bad day".
> You reckon you're having a bad day,
> try missing one – you're dead.
> Any day above ground is a good one.

> Be bloody grateful you woke up this
> morning, lots of buggers didn't.
> I'm grateful I woke up.
> I no longer have bad days, although
> I sometimes have bad *moments*.

I'm also grateful I live in Australia. Fair dinkum, it's one of the greatest countries in the world. I hear people saying: "It's hard!

It's hard!

It's hard!

It's hard!"

You reckon it's bloody hard, go to Bangladesh, go to Bosnia, go to Timor, go to Somalia, go to Zimbabwe, go to Iraq!

I get over to New Zealand quite often, I tell them, "You buggers live in the second-best country in the world". Well, they don't like that.

I don't see boatloads of people leaving Australia heading to Afghanistan.

We live in the luckiest country in the world.

CHAPTER EIGHT

COME TO BEECHWORTH

> *History is what draws the tourists; history is what is debated in Council chambers. The past, represented by Ned Kelly, gold nuggets and iron lace, is put on display.*
>
> **Tom Griffiths, Beechworth, An Australian Country Town And Its Past**

Today, my definition of success is being able to live the life I choose – and I choose to be a baker in rural Australia. That is success for me today.

When I was in Western Australia, people would say I was a great baker who had an incredibly successful business and that I made a lot of money in a little town, but I didn't feel I was a success. I didn't feel I was a great baker, I had a low self-worth and I had a 'poor me' attitude, I felt I was inadequate because of my education and my wrong pronunciation of lots of words. What I couldn't see was that people didn't judge me on those things, I was the only one judging myself. And people don't judge me today. (Though they often do when I'm on stage.)

I am a good baker. Ben Tas said so, Carol said it too and so did a whole lot of other people if I'd only cared to listen. Back in Maningrida days, Jim even said I was a good teacher. Sure, I have a problem working out percentages, but I can work them out in my own way. I used to say: "I can't use a calculator, I can't use a computer." After hearing me saying that over and over, Sharon got sick of it one day and said: "What bullshit Dad, you haven't even tried!" She caught me out.

As time passed I could see that I couldn't lead a balanced life hiding away from society, keeping away from the bakery, and having endless pity parties moaning about poor pitiful me. I started to pop my head out the door and I noticed there was sunshine out there, I started to focus on the positives and for the first time after Carol left, I felt at ease. I felt, "Beechworth is where I belong".

Today, I travel a lot but Beechworth is my home base and I'm happy to admit that I'm going to be buried in Beechworth, but not for a long time - despite my driving. Although I may live in other places, I won't sell my property on the Stanley Road 4 km out of town, I'm going to keep it – this place is my home. I'm going to see the trees grow that I've planted. I'm going make this garden even nicer. It's wonderful to feel that belonging, that the grass isn't greener on the other side. What a wonderful feeling to have this happiness, this wow in my life! Christine has had a lot to do with that, as do my children: Sharon, Kate, Peter and Matthew, and my energy-charged grandchildren.

DIVORCE/REMARRIAGE

Somehow I had turned my head around and I was beginning to experience a bit of a re-birth. One reason was that Christine was writing me all these letters from London where she was working as a nanny. She had been in a relationship in Melbourne after we broke up, but at this point of time she wasn't in a relationship. Meanwhile, I was back in Australia being a single parent, bringing up my two daughters, getting my life and my business together, and thinking about her.

Christine was stable, predictable and very caring. She had a lot of empathy, a lot of awareness and she was very open-minded. I'd hurt Christine a lot. Her letters weren't love letters – no way in the world. They were basic and newsy. Reading between the lines I could see she must have been thinking: "I'm not getting mixed up with that crazy bugger again!"

Christine was also 'normal'. She didn't want to swing from the chandelier or anything like that. She didn't want to react to my over-reactions. Nowadays, when I come home all steamed up about something, she doesn't want to argue and fight. And when we eventually got back together, I found that part of her personality very difficult. In the Toole family, who yelled the loudest, won.

Christine didn't automatically move in with me; I had to court her and all that.

I had to *work* for her!

It annoyed me!

Courting is bloody hard work!

She didn't want to repair me. Before she was going to be Mrs O'Toole she wanted me to sort myself out and to figure out what I was going to do with my wife and all of that.

After attending the self-help course, I said to Christine: "I'm going to start writing down my goals."

She said: "You silly bugger, you're doing it now." I didn't realise that my dreams and my wish-list were my goals. And that's what I know today: *goals are just dreams with a date.* That's all goals are and I was already doing it! I was scribbling what I wanted on bits of paper, but when I started writing the date, boy that changed my whole life because it kept me real focused. I wanted a vintage car and now I've got five of the buggers!

Christine helped me lots and lots, especially by encouraging me and not putting me down. Here I was with someone who believed in me. *Me!* - someone who often didn't believe in himself!

Rather than carrying on about all the things I couldn't do. I started to face up to my real social worth. Some people believed I was a good baker! Others relied on me for their wages! I owed it to these people to have a belief in myself. I owed it to Beechworth. I owed it to Keith. I owed it to my counsellor. I owed it to my employees – and most of all, I owed it to my family.

This poem helped. It's called 'The Man In The Glass':

THE MAN IN THE GLASS

When you get what you want in your struggle for self
    And the world makes you king for a day
    Just go to the mirror and look at yourself
    And see what that man has to say

    For it isn't your father or mother or wife
    Who's judgement upon you must pass
    The fellow who's verdict counts most in your life
    Is the one staring back from the glass

Some people may think you're a straight-shooting chum
    And call you a wonderful guy
    But the man in the glass says you're only a bum
    If you can't look him straight in the eye

He's the fellow to please, never mind all the rest
    For he's with you clear up to the end
And you'll pass your most dangerous, difficult test
    If the man in the glass is your friend

You may fool the whole world down the pathway of life
    And get pats on your back as you pass
    But your final reward will be heartache and tears
    If you've cheated the man in the glass.

I met the writer once.

He had big cauliflower ears.

YES CAROL, I FILED FOR DIVORCE

Earlier, when Carol had wanted me to divorce her, I said, "I'm never going to divorce you" but in the end I made the decision and I filed for divorce. *If it's to be, it's up to me.*

Carol wrote to me from Fiji to say she wanted a settlement and I thought about it and figured: "Well, I'm not going to do a bloody settlement without having a divorce." She came back to Australia and when we went for the settlement the Judge announced: "This is a divorce."

Carol said: "No, we're not getting divorced?"

I said: "Yes, Carol, I filed for divorce. It's no good doing a settlement without a divorce."

The divorce took place on 25 September 1985, and I must admit Carol was more than fair. She didn't 'go me' for everything. Although I had to pay her a fair bit of money, she let me keep the home, the kids and the business. At that time I was in a bit of debt, which I shouldn't have been. That was the price I had to pay for losing the plot.

Carol actually offered to loan me money to help me out of my difficulties – how about that? I didn't take up her offer because I had to break those ties.

About two weeks later she met her future husband and moved in with him. She ended up re-marrying before me, and we've remained friends. She has now been married four times. I hope she finds what she's looking for.

LOVING BEECHWORTH

I learned to love Beechworth. Well, I always did love Beechworth, but until I learned to love myself I couldn't *really* love any place. I love Beechworth – the old gold mines, the beautiful gum trees....

I didn't remain in Augusta – yet I loved the clear ocean, the beautiful beaches, the Kauri trees, the Peppi trees, the Jarrah and the rocky crags. I loved Tocumwal. I loved the Northern Territory – but the love always wore out because I messed up and did things I didn't like about myself. I'd lose my temper, I'd get angry, I'd burn a few bridges, but when I learned to love myself it changed my whole life. Only then did I learn that I could love Christine.

THE ULTIMATE BAKER

Christine and I got married on 23 August 1986, and suddenly my home became stable. *Yippee!* I could focus on the business again! I had someone to look after Sharon and Kate because, honestly, the hardest job I've ever had in my life is being a single parent. It's even harder than thinking! Even today I find it hard to be a responsible parent – Christine's always going crook at me for acting crazy. I've never grown up; my kids think I'm mad. It's normal for me to jump around and annoy everybody. I'm the biggest kid in the house.

Eventually, I bought out Philip, as well as Allan's interest in the bakery, and I was back in there. I reverted back to normal, which (for me) was flat out. I didn't stop to get balance into my life. I was back at 100mph, doing heaps of hours, making up for lost time – I had a lot of catching up to do.

I got totally committed. I got all this stuff out of my head about wanting to own a caravan park or a fish farm, and everything like that. I got in there focused, boots 'n all; I wanted to be *a baker*! And I wanted to have *the best bakery*. And boy, oh boy, did that realisation take a weight off my shoulders!

I stopped looking at other businesses and I stopped peering into other people's paddocks. I was *happy* to be a baker. It was really good to know what I wanted to be. And today, I know what I want to be: I want to be the ultimate baker.

I was born again! New man! New wife! New life! And then I had to get even more organised. That was very difficult.

I worked really hard and the bakery became successful. I did some creative marketing which really helped. I started getting wacky promotional ideas. And most important of all, I started to blend the bakery into the Beechworth locality through sponsorships and general support for the community. Then my business really started to grow.

I expanded into the shop next door which gave us two entrances. We then created an outdoor eating area on the sidewalk. In 1992 the second storey was opened to the public.

Christine got involved in the business too. She took control of office administration. I even remember taking the books out to her when she was in hospital having our second son Matthew. Here she was having to do the wages between contractions! (I still don't write the cheques.)

I really believe readers are leaders, so I started to read business books. This opened up a whole new world of ideas and got me out of my own backyard. I gleaned lots of new ideas from reading business books. I found myself thinking about every detail of the bakery — from the equipment out the back, to the logo out the front.

I drew the big picture first, so I knew where I wanted to go. But then the bakery grew bigger than I ever thought possible.

GET LOST TOM!

Once I started getting my act back together, I began to believe in the magic of thinking big – so I lifted my horizons. I began to focus on what it would take to get the Beechworth Bakery big enough so I wouldn't have to be in there *doing, doing, and doing it*. I wanted it to be big enough to run without me. When I succeeded I struck another problem: I found I couldn't let go. It took a lot to let go, I must admit.

In 1995, I set a goal that I'd be "made redundant by March 1996". One day we were having a bakery meeting and I was complaining that our productivity was too low. I told them, "Our figures aren't good enough" and I ranted and raved for a while.

In the end David, my production guy, spoke up and said: "Tom, I know how we can lift our productivity."

I said: "How?"

He said: "You get out of the bloody place!"

Wow! Did I fire up! *Bloody hell!*

David said: "Well, you're always on the bloody phone. It messes up our roster. We roster you on – and you're off talking to somebody. You're here, you're there and you're only half a worker. Learn to be a manager, stop being a worker." So I got out.

Two weeks later, somebody was sick and they were short-staffed, so I was back in there for the next three to four months.

Then we had a big staff meeting where they told me straight, and after that I stayed away.

I've been out of the bakehouse since. That freed me up, so I started looking around for ideas on how to spend my time. *Now I've gone and written a couple of books!*

PYJAMA MARKETING

Years ago, while at a conference in America, I heard about a lady who ran a slumber party in her little doughnut shop. All her staff slept over and I thought: "Gee, that'd be a bit risky with our lot." So I came up with something else instead. I said to Christine: "We're going to have a Pyjama Day".

I came back from the States, all excited about this Pyjama Day. I promoted it in the papers, I promoted it on the radio, and I got really excited. Unfortunately, I didn't tell the staff and after repeatedly hearing about it in the media, my supervisor came up to me three days before the event and said: "Tom, no one's very happy about this Pyjama Day."

I said: "What are you bloody talking about? I've got it on the radio! I've got it in the paper! Bloody hell! *Why aren't they happy?* Go find out why they're not happy!"

She came back and said: "None of them wear pyjamas!"

"Oh shit!"

So I went out and bought all these pyjamas for my staff. I got a Capt'n Snooze outfit for myself – a long, red Willy Winkie thing. I took my socks off, left my sneakers on, and ran around the bakehouse like a stick insect, with my skinny white legs and they thought: "The bugger's mad! He's really going to do this!"

I never communicated to my staff *why* I wanted them to come to work in their pyjamas. They just thought I was kinky!

(Do you know the difference between erotic and kinky? Erotic, you use a feather. Kinky, you use the whole bloody chook! We have a few chooks at home.)

It is so easy to go to work in your suit, or in your whites, or in your overalls: but you try going to work in your pyjamas, it really gets you out of your comfort zone. The customers see you and think, "Geez, the inmates are running the place!"

I thought: "Bewdy, they're going to come to work in their jarmies, it's going to be a *sexy* day!"

Well, the only ones who came in sexy negligees were the bloody bakers, the fellas. Bloody hell!

FALSE BUMS

The first Beechworth Bakery Pyjama Day was a riot! It went off really well. I got dressed up too. (I think I hid.) Any customer who wore pyjamas got a free loaf of bread. *You'll be surprised what people will do for a free loaf of bread.* The kids don't want to get dressed in the morning, they're quite happy to come in their pyjamas. Plus they were buying up big. I heard one staff member say: "You'd think the buggers would have had something to eat before they'd come out, wouldn't you?"

We held it on a Sunday. Even though Sunday is one of our busiest days, it's never usually busy early in the morning. We opened at 6 am and had about 60 people queued up outside waiting to come in, mainly kids with Mums and Dads – all in pyjamas! On this day we offered a free hot chocolate and a doughnut, and everybody had a great time.

Suddenly I realised we were attracting lots of attention: I was getting scared because I thought some of them might get a bit carried away. I thought: "What are they going to come in dressed next? Big plastic boobs, bloody false bums?"

On the first Pyjama Day, one of the young guys was adamant he didn't wear pyjamas. I walked in that morning and he had his apron on and this bare bum! Well, I was horrified! Good God, I nearly fainted. And then I realised it was a rubber one. Anyway, we stuck him out cleaning the tables that day. He got so many people out of their comfort zone, he really broke the pattern.

In 1999, I was going to cut out Pyjama Day. We'd been running it for six years and I thought it might be getting a bit stale, but the staff wanted to do it again, and we still do it.

When McDonald's launched their new store in Albury they opened it with a Pyjama Day. Lots of other places have copied us and written letters to me: "Tom, I've heard about your pyjama day and our whole *town* has had one!"

I hate to think what we've started. We can lend them a plastic bum if they need one.

REEDY CREEK JAZZ

For many years we've featured live music every weekend. We've tried all sorts of things – now it's mainly jazz on Sundays.

The first band we hired was *The Reedy Creek Jazz Band*, they're great - we still use them after all these years. I asked around and they seemed to be the most popular jazz band in the district. Plus we use a terrific bush band called *Jigid*.

The bands play on the upstairs balcony because I want people to climb those stairs. The customers hear the music and think: "Shit! How do we get up there?"

I also want to put a good feeling into Camp Street. The music gives the town a real ambience. That happy feeling is good for everybody. It's increased our Sunday takings, and given the whole town a real lift. We never take less than $10,000 cash-over-the-counter on a Sunday, all because of 'that little bit extra'.

IF MY BUSINESS BURNED DOWN

My people *are* the Beechworth Bakery. (Tom O'Toole is the Beechworth Bakery too, but most people don't see Tom O'Toole - you won't see me in the shop.) My business is five per cent technology and 95 per cent psychology and attitude.

You can buy milk and bread anywhere, why buy it from us? It's probably dearer!

There's only one reason anyone would do that, and that's because of *our people;* that's all we have. Lots of customers think it's our product, others say it's the marketing, but you can have the best product and the best marketing, but without good people you're ratshit.

If the bakery had burned down in the Beechworth fires (and my people weren't cooked) we could have bought a bit of equipment and moved across the road or down the street and started the Beechworth Bakery up again with the same people. Yet we think our businesses are all about machines, systems and everything else, but they're really not. Business is pretty simple, it's mostly about people.

I'm one of probably 200 (I don't know any more!) and I'm the most useless one.

QUEENSLAND BLUE

We encourage customers to sample our products because it gives us a chance to talk to them. This is mishandled by Keith McIntosh who sets up a table near the door once or twice a week and leads them all astray. (Remember Keith? The guy who's been my friend since I was 16, and who's been my best man three times even though I've been married twice?).

The greatest sickness in this world today is loneliness; people want to be talked to, and Keith never stops talking. If you reckon I talk bullshit, Keith leaves me for dead. He is a shocker, but the customers love him. He talks to the tourists when they come into our shop after they get off the bus. They forget they are wearing name tags, and he'll say, "Oh hello Mary!"

She'll say: "Do I know you?"

He'll say: "I lived next door to you in…?"

"In Kyneton?"

And he'll say: "Yes, I lived next to you in Kyneton! You must remember me?"

"Oh no, I don't really?"

Keith will then say: "Oh Mary, I'm so disappointed! Well try some of this pumpkin bread, do you like butternut pumpkin or Queensland Blue?"

"Queensland Blue."

And he'll reply: "Then this one's for you" - he'll say that *no matter what it is!* It's all the same bloody pumpkin.

Maybe we'll be sampling Eccle cakes, and customers will ask: "What are Eccle cakes?"

He'll answer: "Eccles are a Tasmanian fruit, grown in the south...." He can get away with it and get a laugh – Keith can.

It's that little bit extra, like the band, the sampling, dress-up days and the Queensland Blue.

It's that little bit extra, yet everybody is out there looking for the big fix.

Big is too hard, forget it. Try a little bit extra instead. *Little things are the only things.* I just ask my staff to "improve one per cent ... per week"; anyone can do that. One per cent has got to be simple.

FLASHING THE FIGURES

There were no secrets in our business. All our staff got to see the figures. I used to stick everybody's wages on the staff noticeboard. I never care if anyone goes through my documents. Everything is accessible to any of our staff.

If we're having a bad week or good week, I'll still put the numbers up. I put up the turnover figures, wages, profit and loss, percentages – the works.

People running other businesses say, "Tom, I could never ever do that" because they fear that the staff might get jealous and try to rip them off if the business is doing well. But I wasn't afraid of that. You can access all the figures for the big public companies, so I can't see any reason why I should be secretive with mine.

Talking about figures, we had a tax audit, which was quite funny, I thought...

ALONG COMES THE TAXMAN

My accountant, Richard Hudson, operates from Perth. He is one of my close friends, and I use him because he did such a good job when we had the Augusta Bakery, and also because I have some property investments with Colin Heath in Western Australia. Richard has been my accountant for 30 years and he's very conservative and ethical.

Some years ago he rang up and said: "Tom the Taxation Department is chasing you." They wanted to know about this Tom O'Toole because our return goes to their Western Australia bureau, where my company is registered. But there's a big Tax Office and investigation branch 40 minutes away, just here in Albury. We'd never had a visit from the Tax Office before and he said: "Tom, they'll be coming to see you personally." And I said: "You look after it. You come over here and you talk to them on my behalf."

Richard said: "They'll want to talk to *you*."

I said: "I'm too bloody busy to talk to them buggers! I'm a baker, I don't know anything about figures."

Richard flew over the day before and said: "Tom, I want to explain a few things to you, Christine and Trisha. This is what they do in a tax audit; this is what the tax department will want to know; and these are the questions they're gonna be asking." But I wasn't interested in their trick questions, it wasn't my department.

If you want your wife to lose weight, have a tax audit. It was a great weight reduction program for Christine. You should have seen her, she worried herself sick for six weeks before they came. I said: "What are you so worried about? Are you keeping somebody on the side?" Anyway, the day came and these two serious-looking buggers came to the bakery.

I was in my whites when they asked to see me. I said: "Come on through." I wanted to introduce them to my staff and show them right around the bakehouse, the storerooms and the shop. I'm proud of my bakery, I was happy to show it off.

They were ill-at-ease with this and said: "Look, we'll just look at the books." So I took them up to the office and I could see that Richard, Christine and Trish my bookkeeper were there ready, so I left them to it.

As they were sitting down, one of the tax guys said: "Is Tom coming back?"

Richard said: "I don't think so, he's baking cakes."

They said: "We want to talk to him."

Sure, I'm a director of the company – but first and foremost I'm a baker! They were free to ask Richard, Christine and Trish, any questions they liked, plus they could look at anything they wanted. I couldn't see why they had to bother me as well. The buggers didn't even tell me how nice the shop was looking!

So Richard came downstairs, found me and said: "Tom they want *you*."

Well, I was pissed off! I was up to my armpits in raisins. I was making Christmas cakes. That's my specialty – we make a couple of thousand Christmas cakes a year, all beautifully done by hand. And I was real busy – "Aw, bloody hell!" So I rinsed the cake mix off my hands, went into the office and faced the music.

These tax audit guys must watch a lot of TV because one of them played the bad 'un and the other played the good 'un. Then one turned to me and said: "Do you take your Toyota in the bush much?"

I said, "No no, I'm way too busy."

He said: "We notice you live on 25 acres, do you have any cattle?"

I said: "No no, one of my staff has got a couple of horses there."

And they said: "Ah-ha! Fringe benefits!"

Richard cut straight in: "Hang on! Hang on!" He didn't want to hear about fringe benefits tax just because I was letting someone else's horses nibble my grass.

They said: "Do you collect coins?"

I said: "No."

But they'd already looked at our personal cheque book and spotted a few purchases for collectors coins. They said: "Ah-ha! Look what we've found here!"

I said: "I don't collect coins, but my kids do. I just buy them a set every now and then, no big deal – and it's all listed in our expenditure."

They said: "Who does the banking?"

I said: "My staff does the banking." (I never even take the money out for a newspaper from my business, because if I can pinch it out of the business, somebody else can.)

Anyway, they said to me: "Tom what do you do with all your money?"

I said, "I put it in me shoes."

Well, when I said that Christine put her hands over her forehead, Richard started sinking in his chair and Trisha didn't know where to look. But these two tax guys, got all excited: "Did you say that you put money in your shoes?"

I said: "Yes."

They were real interested in my shoes. They said: "Why do you put it in your shoes?"

I said: "I don't like banks, I don't go to them. My wife goes to the bank."

(All my life I've always put money in my shoes. I don't now, everything's on cards. It's been that way since I embarrassed Christine in front of the tax men.)

They said: "Where do you get the money from?"

I said: "My wife asks me if I want money and I never say no."

They said: "How much is in your shoes right now?"

I said: "I don't think there's any." I really didn't think there was, but a few weeks later I had to go to Portland for one of the first public speeches I'd ever done, and when I tried to pull my shoes on – shit, I couldn't get my foot in there. I reached in and pulled out all this money. I should have told them.

They spent all day there. When they found out a lot of my income came from property deals in Western Australia, they lost interest. We didn't mind. We didn't want them to come back, because they're pretty heavy sort of guys and they make lousy conversation.

THE BREAD LINE

I used to think that if I had money, I'd be happy. Today I know that there's a lot more to life than money. Don't get me wrong, I like having money. Money gives me choices. But good relationships are more important, and I think we have achieved that at the Beechworth Bakery. Staff members have a lot of fun with each other. It's not a business where you get to stand around hoping somebody's going to give you something to do. There's always plenty to do, and when there's plenty to do, time flies and you're never bored.

If you've got time to lean, you've got time to clean, Ian told me that one.

Two deep is too deep. I pinched that from McDonald's. But that's okay for them, the Beechworth Bakery gets five deep sometimes, so what do we do then?

I try not to be manipulative or cunning, I think we run our business ethically and honestly.

After my first birthday in the business, I ran an ad in the local paper thanking everyone for their support. I told everyone the truth, that lots of dramas had happened – like the break-up of my marriage. I was pretty candid and I found that telling everyone the truth, or whatever they wanted to know, seemed to work. So that gave me the idea to keep on opening up my life. I gradually started to write an in-house staff newsletter after hearing somebody talk about how positive it can be for morale.

I started to write things down as they occurred: my marriage, their marriages, fun evenings, everybody's gossip, plus whatever is on my mind. It also gives me a vehicle to say 'thank you'. And that candid approach has become the basis of my newsletter, which I enjoy writing for my staff. It's that little bit extra - for them!

Through our *Bread Line* newsletter, we try to keep our staff fully informed about latest developments, comings and goings and whatever else is in the pipeline. It's more important than ever now that we've got six stores.

We've been running that newsletter for years.

I thank my staff for the great job they do: I tell them what my goals are, what's happening in their lives, where the bakery is going, plus I share with them the newest ideas that I have picked up from: reading books, other newsletters and my visits to other bakeries. I also share the customer comments so my staff get direct feedback – and that motivates them, I believe. These days Marty and his managers are the main ones that write the newsletter

TALKING ABOUT THE BAKERY

Nowadays, my life has changed in a most unexpected and dramatic way. I conduct talks all over Australia and overseas, which is a bit of a worry because they mightn't understand the strong Aussie flavour of my speech.

All I talk about is the Beechworth Bakery and my philosophies about this business. I honestly believe that *business is so simple that most of us miss it.* We get so tied up in complicated theories that we forget that the only thing the customers want is for staff to:

- Look at me.
- Greet me.
- Talk to me.
- Thank me.

That's how simple it is; instead we avoid eye-contact, we keep our bloody heads down as if to say: "Shit! Can't you see I'm busy – get some other bugger to serve you." That sends out a terrible message to customers and yet this is precisely what so many businesses call 'customer service' today. They think cleaning the place is more important than talking to customers.

Git out there! Go to the customer! Work for the customer! You're baking for the customers, you're not baking for the freezers!

I tell my staff: "I'm not paying your bloody wages! Where am I going to get the money from? *They're* the bastards paying your wages! Just look after the customers!"

There are only three rules in our place:

- Rule one – take care of the customer.
- Rule two – take care of the customer.
- Rule three – take care of the customer.

It takes months to find a customer. It takes seconds to lose one.

COME TO BEECHWORTH

We give our leftover food to the Youth Centre, to disadvantaged groups, schools, the Bicycle Club, the Blood Bank and anybody in need.

We let upstairs be used for meetings any time, free of cost to *any* groups. Any groups at all – the Information Centre recently held one there, so did the Chamber of Commerce. If anyone says, "Can we use upstairs for a meeting?" we say, "Sure!"

Sometimes we have to cater for them, but usually they just want a meeting room.

The bakery also gets involved in group TV advertising with other Beechworth businesses. We'll go in with the Lolly Shop or Beechworth Boudoir or the Emporium. The Bakery also supports the Harvest Festival, the Beechworth Celtic Festival, and any festival in any way that we can – with money, food, publicity, and whatever gets people to visit Beechworth.

If we can get them to Beechworth we've all got a chance of getting a dollar out of their pockets. And the only way we can get them to Beechworth is collectively.

GOOD BUSINESS

At times we physically can't get more people into our shop and we upset a lot of customers because they can't get instant service. Well, geez – they've got to wait because there's hundreds of customers. Not one hundred, but hundreds!

Despite the fact that we can seat over 200 people, customers often complain that they can't get a seat, while at the same time there might be another hundred people at the counter waiting to be served: I've counted them.

Well, I haven't counted them – I've had other people count – but there's been 100 people waiting to be served (upstairs and downstairs) with 200 people sitting down. Isn't that incredible, in a little town with a population of around 3000?

When I started this bakery for the second time, we carried about 80 basic lines – we weren't doing coffees, we weren't doing sit-downs, so the lines have increased a lot over the past years. We say we carry 250 lines, but who's counting?

Lots of people come to the Beechworth Bakery from Albury-Wodonga and Wangaratta, but many also travel from Melbourne when they're visiting north-east Victoria. We actually took more than $36,000 cash over the counter in one day breaking our previous record of $32,000. I must admit that was total chaos. Some days we only take $5000. We often take $15,000-$17,000 – I must admit *that's* overtrading too; $13,000-$14,000, that's hard work, but we can do it with a bit of perspiration. But when we're getting up around $17,000-$20,000 we are pushing-pushing-pushing.

We can do the product but it's hard work physically handling that amount of people coming through the door. Most of our lines are in the $2-$4 bracket – a lamington, a meat pie, a cream donut … and we're turning over $17,000 or $20,000 or $10,000 in a day. That's a lot of physical work and a lot of manual labour.

People say, the only working gold mine in Beechworth today is the Beechworth Bakery.

TOP OF THE CROP

One the greatest highlights of my career was winning the 1994, 1995 and 1998 most significant regional attraction in the Victorian Tourism Awards.

Here's how it came about: Robyn Golder, who I contracted in 1994 to do some marketing, got my staff involved and together they decided that we should enter these awards. Well I was in my dream-taker mood, and I was not happy. I thought: "What a complete waste of time and money." But they did it anyway.

Then they told me that we were in the running as finalists, and the big award night was coming up and I had to go. And then they capped it off by saying I had to wear a dinner suit. Well I carried on – as I do – I whinged and moaned. I wasn't going to attend any award night. This was not my cup of tea at all.

It was held in the Melbourne Entertainment Centre with 1800 guests, all dressed in their bloody finest. I felt like a fish out of water, and I was sitting next to Christine – who was radiantly glowing – and I felt pretty stupid. I wished I was wearing my whites instead of a penguin suit.

I felt self-conscious because the category we were in was so highly contested. We were up against the Ballarat Wildlife Park, National Wool Museum, Wilson's Promontory National Park, Victoria's Open Range Zoo at Werribee. We were up against the best in the state. I didn't think we even had a look-in, and next minute they called out the winner, "The Beechworth Bakery!" Talk about WOW!

Here I was
      on stage,
            holding Christine's hand;
                they stuck the mike
                in front of me
        and I didn't know what to say.
      So I just invited them
to all come to Beechworth.

Winning that award was one of the best things that ever happened to the Beechworth Bakery. It really took us into another dimension. It got us right out of our comfort zone. We were now 'up there'. We had something to live up to.

Climb
as
high
as
you
can
dream.

Why not?
And why not now?

BREADWINNER

CHAPTER NINE

OUR FUTURE

*You can't help the poor
by being one of them*
Abraham Lincoln

A lot of people have said to me: 'Why don't you go into the big towns? Why don't you take the bakery to Melbourne? Why don't you go to Albury?' I used to answer 'Albury is too big for me'. In December 2004 we opened a Beechworth Bakery in Aubury. Plus a few more.

In 2001 I sold part of our business to a few of my staff but I had to buy it back because they didn't have enough mongrel in them. Today Marty Mattassoni and his wife Jo are our partners. They have the energy, drive, enthusiasm and skills to take the Beechworth Bakery to the next level. And boy Marty really has that commitment, passion and he's got more discipline than I ever had. They own a big part of the business and their balls are on the line just like mine. They've got their whole future tied up in the 'Beechworth Bakery' brand.

One ship one captain and Marty Mattassoni is the captain, I'm not even a rower. Marty and his managers run the show, they don't really want me butting in on day-to-day things but do seek my opinion, and Christine's, at times. He sets high standards by helping people do the impossible.

I said, 'What's my job?'

Marty said, 'Tom, your job description is the founder'. So I'm the 'founder', it sounded pretty good until he said, 'You're like Colonel Sanders, you're the cardboard cut-out figure, and you're dead!'

Give them ownership, and that's very hard for me because it's been my baby. It was my business and Christine's. I'm seen as the big guru but today I keep out of everyone's way, I'm redundant. Up until December 2004 I made all the Christmas cakes, I've even lost that job. There was a big turnaround in my thinking. Now they make decisions and I think, 'Geez I wouldn't do it that way, oh god almighty!' They don't even ask my opinion, it's their opinion that matters because if they make a decision, they'll make it work. Boy oh boy, what better empowerment is that?

LOTS OF BAKERIES

Boy oh boy we had big plans, huge plans. We wanted 50 bakeries all around the country but reality hit. Fifty – 50! – Beechworth Bakeries throughout Australia. Talk about dreaming big! A bit too big.

And what for?

A reality check isn't a bad thing at times. Right now we have six stores in all, Beechworth, Echuca, Albury, Bendigo, Ballarat and Healesville. It's all right to get there, but to stay there – that's hard. Our biggest goal these days is to grow the existing bakeries to be as famous in their own right as the Beechworth Bakery, and they are succeeding. Albury is a $1 million business, so that's on the way.

And the others are even bigger. Beechworth Bakeries is currently a $10+ million business.

Hire people smaller than yourself and your achievements will be small. Hire people greater than yourself and they'll scare the shit out of you! Marty is younger and really wants to make his mark too.

We can't lower our standards, we've got to raise our standards all the time. We always need that peak-productivity and creativity. We can't have any half-hearted efforts. Don't be scared to demand excellence from your people. Marty and his managers hold people accountable. Marty says, 'These are the figures, this is what I expect' – that's where I used to fall down. Like Christine, Marty has a real grip on figures and strategic planning. It's great having people around to save me and make me look good.

We also reward people. The Beechworth Bakery have sent staff to New Zealand, America, Germany and even up the road to Echuca. Some have never been on a plane, others have never been out of Australia. One didn't even know she needed to have a passport to go overseas! I'd love to send a couple to Zimbabwe, they'd be a little more grateful then!

We always hire for attitude. You've got to have people who are committed to excellence, you've got to have people like Holly, Robert, Janet, Diane, Matt, Sue, Belinda, Annie, Anthea and Jo. It's essential that you have great staff. Without these people there is no hope for the Beechworth Bakery. You've got to have people who are committed - what other criterion is there? If they're committed to excellence you can't go bloody wrong. Christine and my relationship with Marty and Jo is all based on trust. We've got to trust each other and I'm going to back them, I'm going to build them up. That's my job today.

BEECHWORTH BAKERY ALBURY

There's nothing permanent except change. And I've got to be prepared to change my mind. The Beechworth Bakery is growing. I would never have thought that I would have had one in a shopping centre, and then we opened our 3rd shop in Centrepoint, Albury. We bake the product in Beechworth and deliver it fresh every day, so we had to buy a truck. It's very different to the way we were used to doing things at Beechworth, but like I say, you've got to get out of your comfort zone. Customers love it.

I thought, 'This isn't what the Beechworth Bakery is about!' It's totally different, at Albury we had to do a different mix. Who'd ever believe the Beechworth Bakery would be doing this? Oh, boogie boogie boogie boogie! Scary for Tom O'Toole. I've got to feel the fear and do it anyway.

It's been a huge success and it's getting better every day. Wow!

We've given free coffee vouchers to lots of regional businesses. When other business customers aren't sure about buying their product (bed? fridge? computer?) they send their customers down to us and say, 'Have a complimentary coffee and a think, to help you make up your mind'.

We've now got four vintage bakery vans which we drive around the different towns handing out coffee vouchers, participating in festivals and parades, visiting retirement villages and keeping a smile on people's faces.

I was on the Bert Newton Show the day we opened in Albury. The news of our opening went on national television. I was there on the right day, it just happened that way.

We took in excess of $5000 on our first day and there was no grand opening. We dreamed the bakery would take in excess of $1 million a year turnover - without selling bread (because we're next door to a Baker's Delight). And we did! This was all cakes, coffee, sandwiches and pies - we're fairly famous for our pies. Gloria Jeans is just 30 metres away and there's lots of competition. You've got to love your competitors. We're no threat to Baker's Delight, they have their point of difference, they do a great product at a great price. Gloria Jeans are very good on coffee, I'm impressed with their fit-outs, they're brilliant. We're just infants, but we've got a good brand. However, we're not going to stay infants.

We're going to be doing different stuff. Our bloody staff always seem to be dressing up and celebrating something. Every one of our bakeries do a big birthday week of celebrations. We still do Pyjama Days and Kindy Month (August) has become a big thing – our greatest asset are these little buggers and I've got to get them used to bringing in their Mums and Dads. Every day throughout August and even into September we have a group of Kinder Kids in the bakery making cakes and bread.

COMING OF AGE

The Beechworth Bakery is just coming of age, we are now getting out there and walking the talk. We'll only get one shot at growing this Beechworth Bakery, we've had it for years, now it's time to bloody grow. People say, 'you can't change'. We can change and that's what we're doing, we're growing our business.

I'm not suggesting that we've got all the answers, we're far from perfect, we've got lots of learning to do.

We've got to keep asking ourselves, 'Are we still doing the things that made us successful in the first place?' We've got to stick to the fundamentals – fresh product, a great range, great tasting food and terrific customer service. We are doing more training and more leadership courses than we ever did before.

What got us there is not going to keep us there. We've got to keep learning, innovating and welcoming fresh ideas.

We've got Beechworth, Echuca, Albury, Bendigo, Ballarat and Healesville and I'm sure we'll have another one or two down the track if we feel like it. Climb as high as you can dream – why not? Life's a stage on which we have a lifetime to perform, and it's so easy to be negative, it requires no bloody effort. Well Christine, Marty, Jo and I plan to be positive, it's made us as successful as we are today and I reckon it's going to be our secret recipe into the future!

We decided to make some changes and one of them was to cut out milk shakes and iced coffees because we thought, 'If we're not doing them great, we're not going to do them'. So we stopped doing them. We made a big mistake. We forgot to listen to the customer, so we brought them back – and today we're doing them great. In business you can't afford to stop listening to the customer – they'll tell you whether or not your're doing them great!

BOOTS N ALL

We jumped into franchising our Beechworth Bakery brand a little bit too early. We did it in January 2005, in Echuca. Our franchisees were a young couple who did a great job. They put their house on the line and were willing to be part of our winning plan. At the time people said, 'you should never put your house on the line'. My house has always been on the line.

But after a few years they got tired. We ended up buying the franchise back in 2010 and the bakery is still booming. We have no plans at the moment of getting back into franchising.

Complacency, that's our enemy. People say, We mustn't get *too* complacent'. What's this TOO? We can't get complacent at all! People used to say, 'Tom, you're going into Albury, you're crazy, you're going into bloody Bendigo! How do you know it's going to work?' There's no certainty. If there was certainty, we'd all be out there doing it. There is no certainty in life and I know that.

After we become successful we can't stop dreaming, and I've committed that error, I've stopped dreaming, and these guys are pushing me. Marty and his team sometimes scare the hell out of me but if we stick with the basics (*they want it fresh and they want it now*) we can't go wrong.

It's about that enthusiasm – some people have it for 30 seconds, some people have it for 30 years. Great leaders have great enthusiasm, enthusiasm is contagious. If you have enthusiasm for what you do, your staff is going to love your vision for the future.

```
It's about getting out of bed,
    being in love with life,
  it's about being a leader,
    it's about not letting
       TV rob you of life,
 it's about having a great time,
 it's about making up your mind
    to be happy in your skin.
```

THE ELASTIC IN YOUR UNDIES

Like the elastics in your bloody undies, once your mind's been stretched it can never go back to the same level again. You've got to keep stretching.

The Beechworth Bakery Echuca stretched me, and it stretched Marty. The Beechworth Bakery Echuca is growing so dramatically and I believe in time it will beat Beechworth. They doing great things over there.

Marty started with me as a skinny-legged little 13 year old boy. To see the growth in Marty! He's now in his 30s and is our partner in the business he has grown so dramatically he's getting a little bit of a paunch on him. He's in there boots and all, no ifs or buts or doubts or if-onlys, he's in there. You've got to be totally passionate. Not a little bit passionate, not a little bit pregnant – he looks a little bit pregnant sometimes, I can tell you. Marty is terrific, honest, ethical and has no hidden agendas

Healesville was supposed to be our second one, but it wasn't. You've got to be prepared to change. We had lots of problems with Healesville because it's a body corporate, but people are not concerned about your problems, they've got so many bloody problems themselves they couldn't give a stuff.

I can guarantee that Marty is going to make mistakes, but mistakes are life.

If you're not making mistakes you're not really trying, you've got to make bloody mistakes that's how you learn. Oh, and did I make mistakes! One of my mistakes was I had people in as partners who weren't compatible to where we wanted to grow, so that was a big mistake but it would have been a huge mistake if they were still partners today.

The biggest mistake, is to not admit that you've made one.

When most people make a mistake they say things like, 'I had a partner once, I'm never having one again'. Rather than blame the idea, I just admit my mistake and I try harder next time.

I made heaps and heaps of mistakes. I was lacking in financial know-how and vision. For me to grow I needed people with some really top level business skills and I had to get outside help. I got comfortable and that was another big mistake. I wasn't daring to dream big enough and I started to get complacent. Marty sees the bigger picture – my initial dream of one Beechworth Bakery was at least six times too small.

We've got to keep changing, we need to always be bringing in new products – Tom's Curry Pie, Chicken and Leek Pie, Pumpkin and Hazelnut Sourdough bread, Organic Sourdough, a Turkish bread – wow, people will kill for our Turkish bread.

THE TIME IS NOW

We get out of life what we put in to it. Christine and I put a lot into the Beechworth Bakery over the years, it's now time to reap the rewards and we are totally committed. The past is yesterday's history, we've always got to ask ourselves, 'What's important NOW?

The Beechworth Bakery has got the brand out there, we can't waste it – we've got to go with it.

What's important now is that our people have a great leader. And I think Marty and his managers are great leaders and they're teachable. They're tough, hard, motivated, enthusiastic, ambitious and they're in a hurry.

They say, 'The time is NOW Tom. You might get hit by a bus – we want to get a bit of value out of you'. Even though I'm a cardboard cut out figure they want a bit of value out of me. That's nice.

For well over two decades the Beechworth Bakery brand has been built and they're hungry to push this brand out there NOW. Recently I had a phone call from New York from the editor of an American food and travel magazine. She sent a photographer and a reporter to the Beechworth Bakery. We were also written up in a couple of Singaporean magazines because what we are doing in this little rural town in Australia is pretty incredible. *Good Weekend* magazine, wrote an amazing story about us which is on our website. I was on the Bert Newton Show three times in 2004. In 2005 we were written up in the *Book of Success* alongside Alan Fels, Michael Edgeley and some bishop or cardinal. In 2008 I did lots of radio stuff. What's important is that we push our brand out there. Don't wait five years or two years, the secret of getting ahead is getting started – and the time is now.

Dreamers do not quit. And the people who have stuck with us are reaping the rewards – Diane Forrest, who's been with me since 1980 when she was 16 (she's left a couple of times when she's seen me be a seagull manager) and Diane is now our Production Manager. Then there's others who are growing too because they have dreams and goals and it's wonderful to see this happening. Most of us don't dream big enough and then we die. Marty's original goal was to be an owner of a Beechworth Bakery, he's now one the gurus, one of the Grand Pooh-Bahs! He's up there on bloody primetime TV, he's on the radio. He's had a Prince of Brunei at the bakery. Because they're beating the Beechworth Bakery drum, these guys are meeting royalty!

I realise the importance of my brand but I also realise the importance of people with passion, zeal and vision. *People* are probably our brand. What's important now is that we get great people to come on board with us. You've gotta dream big. Dreamers move the world, and Marty and Jo have a big dream. They've got a bigger dream than I had. They're pushing me, they've got me out of my comfort zone, I'm not old anymore, I'm young! I'm young!

We want partners who are hungry, who have a vision, who have passion, who believe in the product and who want to give great service. I want all our team to be successful, because if they're successful I'm going to be successful.

GOALS

I've got to keep stretching myself. After a while the goal board becomes a bit embarrassing because the things that were once hard become too easily achievable. I had a goal that I'd go to Alaska. I've been to Alaska. I had a goal that I'd do the Blue Lagoon Cruise. I've dunnit. And when you get a bit of money you think, 'Geez I can buy that car'. I've done that too.

I've got to keep re-setting my goals. I've got to set great goals. I've got to set goals that will make a difference in my life and in my family's lives. I've got to keep setting goals that stretch me and make my heart sing.

In 2002 I was doing 60-70 paid talks a year, and I set a goal that I'd do 100 in the next year, well I only got to 92. Then in 2004 I did more than 100. And today I still do around 100.

My biggest goal is to see the Beechworth Bakery grow and to see people grow with passion, commitment, enthusiasm, drive and with wonderful *wonderful* attitudes, that's what I want to see. I want them all to have big dreams. Amazing for a guy like me, a kindergarten drop-out with low self worth.

Stop Tom! Don't talk like that!

I shouldn't keep questioning my ability, and you shouldn't question yours. I've got lots of talents and abilities, and I must use them wisely in my speaking. You've got to keep thinking, 'We're the best!' Marty keeps pushing 'Beechworth Bakery, Australia's Greatest Bakery' and I'm thinking oh shit, Australia's *greatest* bakery? But he's right and I'm wrong. We've got to keep having that belief.

We've got to keep cultivating that self-confidence, you've got to taste that victory. Every time I do a talk and I do it well I always think, 'Wow!' I always pray that I can just help just one person. If I help more, it's a real bonus.

You've got to visualise your success before it happens, *The Power Of Imaging* by Norman Vincent Peale is one of my favourite books. I've read it three times and I'll read it again.

Because I'm speaking here and speaking there, one of my problems is I'm getting busier. Over the past 3-4 years we've sold thousands of *Making Dough with Tom O'Toole* DVDs. And we did a new one, *Drop Everything For The Customer,* they're selling like hot cakes and we're getting great feedback. And people tell me that my latest one, *Dare to Dream* (about goal setting), has made a big positive impact on their business and personal lives. And what more could a guy like me wish for – helping people, that's better than making money and even better than making bread.

Our recipe book, *Secrets Of The Beechworth Bakery* has been reprinted and updated several times, it's a beauty. It's bigger and better. People just love it. And I still get letters every week about *Breadwinner,* which I answer. It's a big job.

Goals are about visualisation. You've got to visualise your life. When you wake up in the morning you've got to wake up with that I'm-gonna-win feeling. It's about waking up being in love with life and rarin' to go and asking yourself, 'What do I need to accomplish today to push me to my long term goal?' When you wake up, look ahead with wonder, hope and confidence. Be in awe of life.

If spring only came once every five years, we'd be in awe - but we get it every year and we just take it for granted. We can do that with customers too.

You've got to have that wonder, 'I *can* make a difference in people's lives'. And we can make a difference to people's lives, just selling cakes. It's that smile, that thank you, that eye contact and that service. If you see someone without a smile, give 'em one. Watch out, you might make someone happy!

I WANT TO SEE THE INCA RUINS

When you look good, you feel good.

I've got to wash my hair.

I've got to clean my teeth – what I've got left.

I've got to protect my self-confidence.

I've got to keep away from the energy-suckers, the dream takers.

I've got to remove the clutter out of my mind (and my office).

I've got to keep raising my standards with our products.

I've got to be a role model. (Who? Me?)

I've got to keep asking: 'Are we committed to excellence?'

I've got to keep asking: 'How well are we doing our job?'

I've got to keep asking about every action I take: 'Is it honourable?'

Will our integrity attract people to the Beechworth Bakery?

Will they flock to our organisation?

Am I committed to training my people? We can't short-change them.

We've always got to be working harder to improve our game.

Anything less than our best effort is bullshit.

Never, ever, ever give less than your best.

Culture is caught, not taught. We've got to pass on our rich traditions to the next generation: and Marty and his team are the next business generation.

Sharon, Kate, Peter and Matthew are the next generation in terms of lineage.

Plus Christine and I now have grandchildren!

My purpose in life is to grow the Beechworth Bakery and to grow myself.

I want to have freedom to do what I want to do, and I want to help people.

I want to speak all over Australia and all over the world.

I want to help Marty and his team.

I want to help the Beechworth Bakeries grow.

I want to help my kids believe in themselves.

I want to be happy in my skin.

I want to see my grandkids be happy.

I want to climb as high as I can dream.

I want to go to Egypt and see the pyramids.

I want to go down the Amazon River.

I want to take Christine to Norfolk Island.

I want to go the Inca ruins.

While I'm alive I want to live – not just exist - live.

I don't want to go to my grave with my music still in me,

CHAPTER TEN

MY LIFE TODAY

God grant me the serenity to accept
things I cannot change,
courage to change things I can,
and wisdom to know the difference.
Reinhold Niebuhr

Now that you've read my book, I hope you have enjoyed the story of my life as well as the key ideas that have not only enabled me to build a first class bakery, but to also rebuild myself. The best investment you can do is invest in yourself. The first thing I do when I wake up is I read something positive in the first 15 minutes before the shit comes in.

I need all the education that I can get, so I try to read a book every fortnight. I only read positive literature. I've averaged one book per month during the past 20+ years, so today I'm probably quite self-educated. You've got to challenge yourself, you've got to lift that bar. Read anything that can help you grow.

Looking back, I never liked Tom Toole.

Tom Toole was never at peace.

Tom Toole had a very low self-worth.

I didn't want to be Tom Toole.

I wanted to be someone else.

Today I'm *Tom O'Toole.*

I've been rebuilt and it all started when I was 32.

FOOTBALL OF FEAR

When Carol left I had a second bite at life because without some sort of crisis, my life would probably have floated along, as there was certainly no financial incentive for me to change direction. You can't drift your way to a better life, you can't drift your way to success, you've got to have a goal-map, and you've got to keep steering in the right direction.

Furthermore, even without that crisis, there's a strong possibility that the Beechworth Bakery could still have been exactly the same success it is today. The only difference would be in me: going to work with a football of fear in my guts and a can of worms in my head, and under those circumstances there would be no peace for me – nor for my staff.

Yet there I was at 32 years of age sticking a loaded gun in my mouth.

People say: 'You didn't *really* stick a gun in your mouth?'

Yes I did.

Other people say: 'You didn't *really* change your name?'

I did, yeah.

A lot of people say: 'Oh but you must *really* know the alphabet?'

I don't.

Not knowing the alphabet is no big deal. I employ lots of people and they all know the alphabet. But it would have been a big deal if I'd pressed that bloody trigger. I wouldn't be here today.

People sometimes say to me: 'Tom, how did you let go?'

I just had to let go, and let God.

Thy will be done, not *my* will be done.

The whole cycle of my life has changed. I used to be a loner and I thought I was a real social misfit. Today I'm part of society, the Shire wants me on their committees, I've been on the executive board at the local Chamber of Commerce (I've even been president!) and I conduct talks everywhere, even in jails.

Sometimes I still retreat into my shell, but most of the time I'm out there talking to people on a regular basis. I attend social functions every week – and that's a lot when you're living in the country. I admit, I don't find social dos real comfortable but I make the effort to get out of my comfort zone. Of course I bitch and moan, but I go. I don't think I'm social, but most people see me as a real social person! *So maybe I have to change my self-talk.*

THE GOOD SIDE OF BUSINESS

One of the best things about running a family business is that you can involve your immediate family and the family of your staff, so your kids and theirs can earn pocket money and are never out of work.

That's how my second daughter Kate saved up, which enabled her to spend a year in Paraguay, where she turned 18. Like her big sister, she is fluent in Spanish. The bakery gave Sharon and Kate an income stream which has enabled them to follow their own lifestyle, and that's how it's working out for Peter and Matthew. However, I am quite happy if none of my kids want to go into the business full-time, because they've got to live their own dreams.

My kids see business in a positive light. Most bakery kids don't see the fun side, they just see Dad tired, cranky and wanting to go to sleep, but I say to my staff: 'Bring your kids along. Show them that we can enjoy ourselves'. We have lots of staff functions which involves the whole family. They see my enthusiasm for the business and - like measles and mumps - enthusiasm is contagious. All my kids have traveled to bakery conferences in Germany, New Zealand and America. They think bakers are great.

I love the bakery with a passion, and I also *tell* myself I love it because I could easily say the opposite.

I could start a pity party right now.

I could say: 'Poor me, poor me - this is such a bugger of a job.

Who wants to get out of bed at 2.00 am?

Interest rates are such a worry!

I've got too many employees!

I've got too many customers!

Poor me! Poor me!'

Instead, I tell myself that *I'm in love with life and rarin' to go.*

I don't want to talk about negative things around the dinner table. I want to talk about the positive things – the funny things that happened during the day.

WHAT THE TURTLE TAUGHT ME

Not only is it important to write down my goals in a little notebook, but because I wrote down my goals in the first edition of this book, I had committed myself publicly to doing the things I told my readers I would do. One of these was to travel around Australia in my 1930 A-model Ford bakery van with my mate Keith, a real highlight of 2001. Not only did I see a lot of places, but all those towns got to see the Beechworth Bakery logo on the van, which generated a lot of publicity and lots of laughs. Spending five weeks on the road, traveling at an average speed of 50 kph with no doors, we got to see a lot of Australia. We also experienced the *smell* of the place – every dead rabbit, every dead kangaroo, 17,000 kilometres of it.

We were lucky to get away with it, so we decided to push our luck. When we'd recovered from our trip I set a new goal – that we'd go to Cape York by the end of 2003, and that's what me and Keith did. Boy oh boy, everyone was shocked when we announced that we were going to drive the A-model Ford to the tip of Australia. It was hard enough on bitumen, but when our regional paper The Border Mail announced our intentions we had people from everywhere telling us we were mad. So many people told us that we would not make it: 8000ks all up including 850 kilometres of dirt corrugation, sand, plus rivers – two aging guys in an aging Ford on a 4-wheel drive only road – did I say 'road'? 'Track' would be too kind. It was bloody tough.

These Good Samaritans would wave us down and say, 'You guys are psycho, you don't know what's ahead!' Other people would wave us down to take photos and they'd say, 'The road gets better...'. They lied, the buggers lied!

On that trip we met so many energy-suckers who told us we wouldn't make it. It's just like in business, the dream-takers told us, 'Tom, the Beechworth Bakery can't work in a shopping centre, it's not a destination'. We met so many on the trip to Cape York who told us we would not make it, and I tell you what – **they were nearly right!**

Going to Cape York was just like being in business. It was hard, and at times so rewarding. We saw jabirus prancing around and thousands of spider webs in the morning dew. What an achievement, to stand on the most northern tip of Australia – and we made it! It's just the same with opening a new bakery. When Marty and the team open a new one they are ecstatic and filled with incredible wonder, just like when Keith and I made it to the tip of Cape York, what a buzz! Set the goals and enjoy the journey.

And the harshness of the trip. There's a lot of harshness in business. Here we were getting our photo taken at the most northern tip of Australia and a big turtle came out of the water, stuck its neck out, looked at us and thought, 'Who are these clowns?'– and that's what you've got to do in business – you've got to stick your bloody neck out, just like that turtle.

They used to call me turtle in primary school. I thought it was an insult, after Cape York I think it's a real compliment – because you've got to stick your neck out.

SECRETS

Another project that I found daunting at the start was my second book, a cookbook titled *Secrets of the Beechworth Bakery.* I wanted to write a recipe book that readers would use in a practical way, I didn't want to write a coffee table book that everyone would be scared to mark with flour and a few ingredients. I like everything to be simple and practical, which I believe we achieved.

I'm no great baker – or maybe I am – I seem to keep changing my mind all through this book, but one thing is for sure, I'm no great baker in a domestic kitchen. My comfort zone is a commercial bakery where I make a couple of hundred lamingtons at a time. I find it real difficult to make a batch of six, and the same applies to loaves of bread.

So I got my head baker to break down all our best recipes. He made each one in his domestic kitchen to make sure they worked for the reader – and we have had a real good reception for my second book.

You've read my story, how could I have done any of this if I had the same head on my shoulders as when I was living in Yarrawonga?

I couldn't. It would have been impossible. If a bugger like me can do it, you can too.

HIGHER POWER

As long as between my ears is all right, it doesn't matter what else is happening. I'm no guru and I've got to be careful that people don't push me into being something I'm not: I'm Tom O'Toole, baker, businessman and country person. I am also a speaker and a writer. I keep telling people: 'I'm not a great speaker and I'm no writer'. It sounds like my 'I'm not a great baker' line.

I'm always telling everyone I'm hopeless, I can revert to my old ways very easily. But I can't be hopeless because I gain strength from a greater power. I've found my place in the universe.

I'm not religious, I don't go to church, but I believe in a Higher Power which I call G-O-D – Good Orderly Direction.

It's a God of my understanding. It's a loving God. I'm not living in fear. *When you're at peace with yourself, any place is home,* and most of the time, I'm at peace with myself today.

Any time I feel guilt, I'm either doing something I shouldn't be doing or not doing something I should be doing. If I'm not being fair, it plays on my mind. I have to clear it up. And that's what living in the *now* has given me. If I can go through life without the remorse and guilt of stealing other people's day – then I'm at peace. And that is success: being at peace.

The prayer that I mainly use is:

God grant me the serenity to accept things I cannot change,

courage to change the things I can,

and wisdom to know the difference.

I couldn't change my mother, I can't change my past, I can't change my staff, I can't change my kids, I can't change my wife, I can't change anyone else. The only thing I can change is me. People can alter their lives by altering their attitudes. It doesn't matter what our past has been, we all have a clean future.

I don't go around telling everyone I believe in God, but I believe there is a Higher Power. There's got to be. There's a universal strength out there. I don't know what it is but I feel much stronger with the knowledge that I'm not alone in this universe.

BORN RICH

One day, when Kate came home from primary school she asked, 'Daddy, are we rich?' and I had to think about that question.

Today I know the answer is yes, we are all born rich, richness comes from within. We are born with two arms, two hands, two legs and we've got this neck-top computer.

I used to say 'I'm just a baker' and I know today that God never made a 'justa'. There's no such word. Everyone of us has skills and talents and I'm not 'just a baker'. I'm a human being with lots of skills. Just like you.

But the dollar still drives me. I love the choices that money gives me. Without money I can't help anybody else. I can't grow my business without money, I can't go to South America without money. I need money to help my family, my kids and to help other people. I do a lot of free charity talks, school talks and self-help talks. People say to me, 'Tom, you don't still do it now for the dollar…' I do! I have got a front door. I am in business. I do it for the dollar, plus I love what I do.

JUST ASK

If you want something, just ask. These words often get me into trouble. I was recently speaking to a group of financial planners. Later, one of them asked if I would help set up a bakery training school in East Timor. It was out of my league but seeing I'd just told them 'just ask' I said I'd see what I could do.

So I got onto my two good mates, Ralph Plarre from Melbourne and Graham Heaven from Napier New Zealand. Both have run their own successful bakeries, both are very busy but both said yes. So we visited East Timor where we were introduced to many organisations and government departments, but we could tell there was going to be no action from that end.

The day we were due to leave, we were taken to a convent run by the Silesian nuns on the outskirts of Dili. The order manages 10 communities in East Timor, including orphanages, tech schools and a clinic. They had an ideal building for a bakery. More importantly they had new bakery equipment, donated from Spain. It was still in the packing crates. Graham got so excited he blurted out, 'We'll help set up the bakery!' (Ralph and I both threw looks at each other, *bloody hell*!)

The three of us were very busy at the time, and we encouraged them to work with an Indonesian baker. He did a terrific job but the nuns wanted to make Aussie bread. So eight months later, in 2011, we went back. Who ever thought I'd be living in a convent? Well, we stayed in one - Mr Graham, Mr Ralph and me - Mr Tom. We ate every meal with the nuns. They prayed before and after the meal. I was getting holier every day!

Boy, some of these people didn't even know how to use their own gear! But the Timorese were keen to learn. They would pick up straight away whatever we showed them. We taught them to make bread and showed them how to get the best out of their equipment.

When we visited in January 2012 - to a helluva welcome! - we could not believe what they accomplished in one year! The bakery now employs 10-plus and is training these young people in hospitality and baking. We showed them how to make lamingtons, savoury scones, muffins, rock cakes and French sticks. They are learning wonderful skills. In my mind, helping set up this bakery is one of my greatest achievements. It was a real challenge but with Ralph and Graham there were lots of laughs.

Last year I was speaking to a community group in the far north Queensland town of Ingham. Maybe I mentioned my baking experiences in Maningrita, maybe I told them about Dili or maybe I said *just ask* - but a church minister, Nino Marolla, was in the audience. After the talk, Nino asked if I could help his team set up a bakery in Uganda. I tried hard to get out of it but in the end I said yes.

I need to be open to new experiences.

The more I give, the more I get.

Nino painted a very different picture to East Timor. No equipment except a small wood oven. No front door on the bakery. Plus (I had to say it) 'it also needs electricity and a dough mixer'. Nino replied, 'Tom, all these people are unemployed'. I insisted, 'I still need a mixer!'

This bakery is to be set up to support an orphanage. It's at Kumi, which I understand as being in the sticks of Uganda. Again, I have asked my good mates, Ralph and Graham to help out.

Though we were all uncertain at first, we're now getting fairly excited. As I write this paragraph - we are heading off next week (April 2012). I hope we can make a difference to these people's lives. A good website that'll tell you all about Uganda is www.cohad.org.au - just follow the links.

EVERYONE HAS FEARS

Nowadays I mix with all sorts of people. I can meet anyone today because I know they're just like me. Everyone has fears, everyone has doubts and everybody gets a little bit low. I'm sure they do.

Every day I work on myself and that's how I cultivate self-confidence. Don't compare yourself to anybody else, we're all bloody different, we all have different dreams. Everyone seems normal until you get to know them. There's no one else like me in the world – god almighty, you wouldn't want to be!

The more I help other people, the more I help myself. I thought I was hard done by because I failed kindergarten, but not long ago I met a guy who said he'd failed recess! There's always someone worse off than you.

Only work with people you like: life's too short to do otherwise. My book publisher Sam the Wog, treats me so good. He's an old pizza maker, he knows what baking is like.

I also work with my speaking bureau ICMI, they manage all my talks. They know I'm a bit thick, they know I can't pronounce lots of words but I love working with them, they're a great mob.

WHAT'S THE SECRET?

There's no excitement in being average. If you're not prepared to get out of your comfort zone and do that little bit extra, you're bloody history. The only way you're gonna get ahead is if you stick your neck out just like the turtle.

Lots of people say: 'Tom, what's the secret?'

Well, there's many different things – like enthusiasm, passion, belief in yourself, belief in your product, belief in your community – wow!

Embrace **WOW** – get **WOW** in your life!

We might have it at work, but then we don't have it at home. We come in and we flop in front of the television – that's not **WOW**. If you don't have **WOW** in your life, why get out of bed?

My life has changed, it really has. Sometimes I reminisce about Tom Toole, a Tocumwal kid, standing near the woodheap with my mate, watching the Murray River going places. And I'd remember knowing that some day my life would be like that river.

HAPPY WITH NATURE: DAD

Life's a journey, not a destination. Yet I always thought it was a destination – get this, own that, and you'll be happy Tom. Then I'd own it and I still wasn't happy. I was always searching and searching, and today I know happiness doesn't come in things, it comes in people.

I always thought it *did* come in things, yet I had an incredible role model in my father. Happiness was in him, he wasn't looking for things. He was happy with nature, with **WOW** – and with all the simple stuff I'd been searching for in my life - yet he always had it all.

I used to think, 'He couldn't possibly be happy, he's too bloody poor', yet he went to work singing and came home singing. It wasn't a put-on, he was in love with life; yet I couldn't be, because I was an angry young man. Bloody hell, I was angry at the world.

My Dad had empathy with nature; now here I am living in the country on 25 acres. I love nature and that is one of my strengths. Maybe I got it from him.

Dad had character defects like all of us. He was a bit of a dirty old man, in lots of ways. Before coming inside the neighbour's wife would yell out, 'Are you home Nona?' because if Chris was home alone, they were a bit wary. And when he was in hospital the nurses wouldn't get too close to him, because he was liable to stick his bloody hand up their dress.

I don't ever want to grow up to be a dirty old man.

BEST IS YET TO COME

I also believe *the best is yet to come*. And boy, that gives me a lot of comfort. I was at this economic conference and the speaker before me told everybody: 'The worst is yet to come!' *The worst!* I couldn't believe my ears! Why would anybody say that? This guy was actually talking about all this incredible horror. Why didn't he just shoot himself?

Well, I believe the best is yet to come.

It's getting better.

I'm getting better.

Every day gets better for me.

More peace, more serenity, more love in my life.

Just one day at a time, it's all I have –

and it's *just for now.*

I don't have to worry about next Christmas or my next birthday, all I've got is *now.* I used to worry so much about tomorrow, but I may die in my sleep - and I'll have wasted all that energy worrying. *Fer what?*

YOUR BLOODY WANKER MATES

Seamus my mate was always gonna learn the fiddle but never doing anything about it. He said, 'Tom, I'm gonna be 54!'

I said, 'You're gonna be 54 *anyway.* If you start learning the fiddle you're gonna be 54 and you'll have learned the fiddle'. So he learned the fiddle. Do you know, he's now teaching kids to play the fiddle and he's only just learned himself! Bloody hell.

It all comes back to that dream. Build the castle in the sky, and then start building a foundation under it. Write down your goals. I've got tell you though: goals do not matter to people who are going nowhere. Put them on paper and go somewhere!

After I said all this in a talk someone came up to me and said, 'Tom, do you really believe all that bullshit?' and I was stunned! I was up there for an hour, pouring my heart out, only to have someone say that! I was shaking, I nearly grabbed him by the throat. I said, 'Of course I do'.

He came up to me a week later and thanked me. He said, 'Tom, you've changed my life. A week ago, me and my business partner were sitting in your audience wondering where we were heading. I'm 55, and I wasn't dreaming big enough'.

Get a life. Get that vision. Invest in yourself. Dream big. Write down everything that you want to achieve, maybe set a goal of 100 things you want to achieve. If it's not on paper, it's not on this planet. Success does not come easy. Nothing worth having comes easy.

Dedicate your life to proving all your bloody wanker mates wrong.

PAYING THE PRICE

Most people are not willing to pay the price.

It's up to me to convert my dreams into goals.

I can't blame anybody else.

I've got to keep visualising my dreams,

I've got to keep them active and I've got to stay focused.

That is the secret, you've got to stay focused on your goals.

I was booked to do a talk in Mount Isa and the plane was running late. At Brisbane I said to Qantas, 'You'll let them know in Townsville that our flight is late…?' and they said, 'Yes, they'll hold it for you'.

But when I arrived in Townsville around 5.30 in the evening this self-important little guy said, 'We let your plane go, you taxied too long on the tarmac' (well, I wasn't driving the bloody plane!). The plane had left 10 minutes earlier without me. But I had to do a 6.30 breakfast meeting in Mount Isa next morning — and I had to get there. I didn't hesitate, I chartered a plane – it cost $3500. If I said I'd be there, I had to pay the price.

My brother 'Mad Mick from Mount Isa' was in that audience. No one knew we were brothers because we've got different surnames. He's Toole and I'm O'Toole.

Mick was so embarrassed, hearing me airing the dirty linen about the family – telling them about the cockatoo that shat a stalagmite, about Mick shooting James with sparrow shot, about me saving up to buy my own bed, about swaggies and bats and Catholics, about not having proper doors on the house and that we never had a bathroom. He was so horrified, he said, 'Tom, I thought I was going to have a heart attack, I went so red'.

And then he said, 'Tom, you inspired me! I got motivated by my little brother!' Wonderful!

EMMA GEORGE

Only when we continue to raise our goals do we give ourselves room to grow. You've got to keep lifting that bar and lifting that bar, that's the purpose of our lives. Most of us get into business and after a while we start dropping that bar or we hold it steady, like I did for a few years.

You've got to lift it that little bit extra.

Beechworth is the home of Emma George, a former world record holder for the Women's Outdoor Pole Vault. Emma won the Australian title and broke the Commonwealth record five times before smashing the world outdoor record in Melbourne. She broke the record a further four times in 1996, twice in 1997, three times in 1998 and once in 1999. She broke the record by jumping 35cm higher than her first attempt, an incredible improvement in four years. And her final win was only fractionally higher than the world record – but that was enough!

Emma understands that little tiny weeny weeny tiny tiny tiny little bit extra can make a world champion!

That's all it is, that

little

weeny weeny

tiny tiny tiny tiny tiny

little little liddle liddle liddle bit extra

– that's all it is!

That *tiny tiny tiny weeny fraction of a centimetre* – it's the little things that make the big difference.

We've got to keep lifting that bar and lifting that bar.

Most success and failure in life is where we set that bar.

Why? Why? Why?

Why not?

If you say 'I can't' - you won't

If you say 'I quit' - you lose

If you say 'I'll try' - you might just win

Only you have the power to choose.

So choose to be happy, you buggers!

They say that a journey of a thousand miles must begin with a single step. A Chinese philosopher said that in 500 BC. You've always got to ask yourself, What steps have I taken today to improve my life? You've got to make sure that your goals are positive and that they are challenging.

You might bust a valve, so bloody hell – get going! 'Here lies Harry, he never died because he never lived.'

I'm going to have on my tombstone: 'Here lies Tom, he just ran out of time'.

When I die I want to still have a bloody big goal list, I want to keep motivated, I want to keep living, I want to – bloody hell, you might think I'm mad, but geez I've lots of go in me.

I'm just getting wound up!

CHAPTER ELEVEN

THE GOSPEL OF TOM

> The first responsibility of a
> leader is to define reality.
> The last is to say thank you.
> In between the two, the leader must
> become a servant and a debtor.
> **Max DePree, Leadership Is An Art**

Who the bloody hell is Tom O'Toole? It took a long time for me to figure out the answer to that question, I can tell you!

I've got pieces of paper everywhere. I write down all the best things that I read – all the sayings and ideas that I think are pretty good. I've pinched a lot of other people's thoughts for this book, but I've lived them and I've really tried to walk the talk. And I've made them my own through living through these ideas, living up to them the best I can.

I suppose, like a re-built motor and after a lot of soul-searching, this is Tom O'Toole. This chapter is who I am – ideally.

People keep asking me, "Tom, what's the
secret?" — well, I don't think there is
just one secret, there are many.
Sometimes I say it's getting up
in the morning in love with
life and rarin' to go.
Other times I tell them,
beware the dream-takers.
Other times I say it's having
that belief, that passion,
that enthusiasm.
Or maybe the secret is what was written
on the back of our old business cards
until my marketer asked me to stop. Our
business cards used to say:
What you'll find at The Beechworth Bakery
is friendly staff, chaos, delicious fresh
product, seating for 200.
It's that little word 'chaos'.

Here are a few of my key philosophies. I'm not saying they're
original, but what is original? Everything you read in books all goes
back to the great philosophers and all that. I'm no bloody business
guru – take what you want and leave the rest - but this is how I try to
run my business:

1. REMEMBER WHAT I TOLD YOU IN CHAPTER ONE

Beware of the dream-takers! Get famous! Get out of your comfort
zone! Take a risk – smile! Enjoy your work! Have goals! Shock
people! Enjoy the journey.

Now that you've read my story, you'll understand why I started
getting into all this positive stuff. It puts energy into situations and

out of it will come a bloody lot of self-belief, which we all need to get through any day.

It's no good sitting in a corner with a bottle of plonk and having a pity party of one, Poor me! Poor me! That's not living.

And it's no good sitting behind a counter and resenting your customers when they come in the door. That's not living either.

Take a risk – smile.

A smile is the quickest way to wreck any pity party. Any time I want to get out of depression I just find someone to help. It gets me out of me.

That's how simple it is.

2. BELIEVERS PICK UP THE PRIZES

Belief radiates energy. Having a belief in yourself is the first step to success. If you believe in yourself, others can believe in you too. They will pick up on your passion and enthusiasm. It's just like dropping a stone in a pond: your belief will ripple out and touch every one.

Maybe you've got to fake it until you make it - well that's okay.

Don't forget that the secret of getting ahead is getting started.

Don't wait until you're bloody organised. Don't say things like, "Tomorrow when I get organised…" - it's crap!

Tomorrow's success begins today.

You're either gonna do it or you're not.

A lot of people don't know what they're on about.

They go: "Can I/Can't I? Can I/Can't I?"

One day they're gonna wake up and think: "Shit, I'm 60 and I haven't had a go yet."

The believers pick up the prizes in this life.

You've just got to believe: "I can do this".

3. NONE OF US IS AS STRONG AS ALL OF US

Together everyone achieves more. When we all work together, we all win together. We're either pulling together or we're pulling apart. The day that everyone achieves less through working together is the day the team breaks up. Just imagine: if you had every element of your business pulling together as one - nothing would stop you.

Sometimes we work against each other in the team, even against our wives or partners, but we lose out because none of us is as strong as all of us.

The future of your business will be a reflection of your teamwork. I want my people to appreciate each other's jobs. All my bakers have to spend some time serving in the shop, so they all experience the stress of working the counter. I don't want the guys out the back thinking: "Front-of-house have got it easy." Boy oh boy, they sure see pressure when customers are five deep, all desperate to give them money – desperate!

Walking the talk: I'm the only one who doesn't work in the shop because I'm frightened of people. I'm terrified of being criticised or somebody saying: "$2.50 for that? It's not worth it!" I don't handle criticism too well. If a customer isn't happy, I'm liable to tell them to piss off and go to McDonald's! (We don't have McDonald's in our little town.)

I'm also scared I mightn't know some of the product lines. A customer might say, "What's in this cake?" and I mightn't be able to answer.

Here's the founder of the Beechworth Bakery, asked the ingredients of a cake and unable to give an answer! Yet I'm out the back preaching to my staff: "You've got to have intimate knowledge! You've got to sell with passion! You've got to give 'em eye contact! Kill 'em with kindness!", and I mightn't have it myself.

4. THE MORE YOU LEARN, THE MORE YOU EARN

I believe that the more you learn, the more you earn and I have proved that with my reading of Small Business Letters and these sorts of publications since the mid-1980s. It's certainly worked for me. Most of us finish our schooling and stop learning, but because I was a kindergarten drop-out I simply had to keep on learning otherwise I wouldn't know a bloody thing! I'm going to be the same person in five years time except for the books I read and the people I meet. Why would you be any bloody different? TV's not going to change your life.

I am very careful about what I allow into my head because you become what you study.

Within the first 15 minutes of waking up, I make a point of reading something positive before the shit comes in. I read a page out of the Norman Vincent Peale book, Positive Thinking Every Day, and I have done so for years. I also read Daily Reflections as well as another Norman Vincent Peale book of thoughts called Have A Great Day – I read it, and I do have a great day!

I believe that if you fill your head with crap, that's what will come out your mouth.

If you study doom and gloom, you'll become doomy and gloomy. You will create a self-fulfilling prophecy. Your income will rarely exceed your personl development. I have to keep investing in me.

Walking the talk: People say to me: "How do you find time to do all these things?" Well, I have one or two hours in my day more than most people, because I don't watch any TV. Television robs you of your life. I haven't watched the news for over 20 years. Why bother? It's the same bloody news as what I was watching all those years ago. The same wars, murders, rapes, doom and gloom, smashes and crashes, bank robberies, all tragedies – it hasn't bloody changed.

However, I read newspapers because I'm in control. I can flip the pages to the things I feel are worth knowing.

5. LITTLE THINGS ARE THE ONLY THINGS

If you are not determined, utterly totally determined to stand out, you're bloody history. There are so many me-too products, me-too businesses you've got to do that little bit extra. That's all it is – that little little liddle liddle liddle liddle liddle liddle little bit extra.

It's not a big deal, it's a smile.

It's not a new patent, it's a detail.

It's not a new shop front, it's service.

It's not tremendous change, it's just a thank you.

It's the little things that make the big difference.

Little things are the only things,

Yet we're all looking for the big fix.

6. THIS LITTLE BIT BETWEEN MY EARS

I used to be convinced that the Beechworth Bakery couldn't grow any bigger, but I was wrong. And today I realise the only thing that limits me is this little bit between my ears. We put our own limits on ourselves. I could easily stand still in my business. It's so successful that I could live happily ever after and take no more risks.

People keep saying, "Tom, you can't grow any more". They were saying that when we were turning over $2 million – now we're turning over $3 million, and I believe we haven't yet peaked!

If I can take $17,000 on a Sunday and $26,000 and $20,000 on record days (and my average is nowhere near those figures) why can't I lift it up on other days too?

I can and will grow more. It's a challenge, I should shoot for the stars and lift this business by another million. Imagine that – they'd be queuing up around the bloody corner and halfway down the street!

Walking the talk: I want to find a way of getting crowds in on Mondays, Tuesdays and Wednesdays like we do on Saturdays and Sundays. Once I can figure the answer to that problem - and it'll be a simple one - then I can take off again. To tell you the truth, for us to grow, we've got to go. That's why we opened a second store in Echuca, a third in Albury, a fourth in Bendigo, a fifth in Ballarat, a sixth in Healesville and that's it for now, but who knows what the future holds?

7. WHAT YOU THINK ABOUT EXPANDS.

I used to be a worrier. Oh God, my guts would be in a knot with worry. Today I don't worry. Worry is just negative goal setting – and why would anyone want to be involved in that?

What you think about expands - that's how former US president Bill Clinton got into trouble.

So think positively! Look for opportunities! Get excited! Talk up the business! Brag about your job!

I tell other business people about our staff training, our jazz band, our range, our promotions and I expect them to get excited too. Then they say: "Great idea Tom, but we haven't got the money or the time." It's crap. If you want to do it, you'll bloody do it. I get a bit frustrated when they can't see that. I share my best ideas and some people shrug it off. Here I am doing their bloody thinking for them, and they don't grow, they shrink! I feel like sticking them in the bloody oven, I do! I like to see people expand!

I tell them it's not lack of time nor lack of money: it's lack of focus and lack of priorities! If you're thinking lack of money and lack of time, 'lack' is all you're gonna get. Lack is slack.

I see a lot of negativity in business:
interest rates and petrol prices are
going through the roof,
rural Australia is doomed,
the bloody drought,
tsunamis and cyclones,
we're finished!
Oh, bloody hell, the sky is falling!'

What you think about expands, and that's why you've got to be so bloody careful what you stick inside your head.

People say: "But Tom, you know what it's like - you were in business during the 80s when we were having a recession." I don't get into that stuff. I tell them I've never participated in one. Who wants to be in a recession? I think these recessions must be good for bakeries, because people might think 'we won't go out to dinner tonight' but they will always be able to afford a treat, like a chocolate éclair, a gourmet pie or something like that.

8. PUT DELEGATION INTO ACTION

When you're placed in charge, take charge. Bloody hell, I don't want to take charge; that's why I'm such a good delegator! But he's right – lead, follow, or git out of the bloody way.

Until I learned to delegate I couldn't grow, and I believe the No.1 reason the Beechworth Bakery can grow today is because I have learned to delegate. Years ago, I read an article on delegation and I said, "I'm gonna try this!" and action was the magic word. I put delegation into action. I now think I'm pretty good at delegating.

Walking the talk: Delegation was very hard for me when I was chief oven man; because I was the one who watched and made the doughs; I was the one who rolled the jam rolls. I was it, and it was all me, me, me, me – small business is like that. I then had to break all those habits, all those ties, and I had to genuinely learn how to delegate because without it, I've got no personal freedom.

If I go into the bakery today, which I rarely do, all my production managers will tell me what to do – they're the bosses. I don't over-ride them or my other managers.

However, they don't always keep me informed. I cracked the shits when they started having supervisor and manager meetings without me. I said: "How come I'm not invited?"

My manager replied: "You own the place, you don't work here. We didn't know we had to invite you."

When I knew I didn't have to be invited, I stopped wanting to go. Now I rarely attend.

But sometimes I will go, especially when they think: "It's time we had a burst of Tom".

I often do far too much talking and not enough listening. I know that when I talk I'm only repeating what I already know, but when I sit and listen, I may learn something.

9. DON'T LET AN OLD PERSON IN

Today, I know if I'm not making time for health, I've got to make time for ill-health. I try to have a healthy routine because I want to live a long life and I want to enjoy it. You don't pay the price for good health, you enjoy the benefits. But I do love cream cakes and all that stuff.

In 1957, Senator John Glenn was the first person to fly across the USA faster than sound. In 1962, he was the first American to orbit the earth in space. In 1998, he returned to space in a space shuttle – up there at the age of 77!

At the same time that he was flying around up there, I went to visit my Mum who was also in her 70s, and there she was going: "Ooh I'm dying! I'm going! I'm going! I'm going!" She was putting little stickers on vases, on the tea pot, and giving away the little jewellery that she had. She was getting ready to die. My Mum had no dreams left and it was really sad to see.

Not long ago an 85-year-old guy told me he was going prospecting. He said: "Next year I'm going to Kalgoorlie." He didn't say, "I hope to", "God willing" or any of that. He simply said "I am going". He hasn't let an old person in.

Old age will only appear when we stop dreaming. Some people are old at 35, others aren't old at 85. Senator Glenn got into that space shuttle and did all these incredible things because he's got all these dreams – which isn't bad for a bloke born in 1921. When you cease to dream, you cease to live.

Walking the talk: You see lots of old people just waiting to go, because they've stopped dreaming. I ran out of dreams too, but today I've got lots of dreams. I wanted to go down the Murray River in a bathtub, dunnit! Over 2000 kilometres in a bathtub! I wanted to drive the A-model Ford to Cape York, dunnit! Next big challenge – the Birdsville Track. I want to build my turnover by an extra million, I want to plant another 10,000 trees on my Rutherglen property.

As I said, climb as high as you can dream – why not?

10. WITHOUT GOOD PEOPLE, YOU'RE RATSHIT

You hear managers saying all the time: "My staff is my biggest asset," but they don't mean it. Well, I do: my people are our biggest asset, because without them we don't have a business. We can't run the business without them. If you believe that people are your biggest asset, you need to invest in them.

Our staff are our biggest investors - they invest their time, their energy and their imagination. Without them we don't have a business.

You can buy your milk and bread anywhere, why buy it from the Beechworth Bakery?

It's because of them.

That's how simple it is, yet we think it's 'our product, our product, our product!' You can have the greatest product plus the greatest marketing, but without good people you're ratshit.

11. THINK GREAT THOUGHTS

Mediocre thinking attracts mediocre results. Great thinking attracts great results. So if you want great results, think great thoughts.

What's your greatest personal asset? Some people think education is their greatest asset. Other people feel that money is going to solve all their problems. I say, your greatest asset is your mind.

I read somewhere: If you keep believing what you've been believing you'll keep achieving what you've been achieving. So raise the stakes: think great thoughts.

Walking the talk: I find thinking, bloody hard work. I find it easier working in the bakehouse: that's my comfort zone, where I don't have to use my brain much. However, I realise that if you want things to be different, the answer is to become different yourself. And that takes a lot of thought. The only thing that limits me is that little bit between my ears.

12. MISTAKES ARE LIFE

Life's like a bike – the harder I peddle the further I go. When I was a little kid, I rode my pushbike up the main street of Tocumwal. In the middle of the main street was a silent cop, and I ran into it and fell off in front of all the people. I broke a few teeth, made a real dick of myself but I hopped back on and rode away. And that's what we should do in business when we fail. Yet when we go into business it's as if our whole objective is not to make any mistakes. Mistakes are life.

I've made heaps of business mistakes. I don't like making them, I can tell you! You feel stupid when you fall off your bike, but you've got to keep getting back on, just like kids do. But in business we're often too cautious, we think, "Oh shit, I'm never going to do that again." And we don't. We don't do anything else either. The best way to avoid criticism is to do nothing, say nothing, be nothing.

13. HIRE FOR ATTITUDE, NOT FOR LEGS

I always say to my managers, "Hire for attitude and train for skills" because I believe that a staff member with a good attitude is three quarters of the way there. It's very hard to change someone with a bad attitude, no matter how many skills they have. I had to change my attitudes – it took a lot of bloody work.

People say: "Tom, what do you look for when you're hiring people?"

I say, "Long legs, big tits!" No I don't.

I say, "Enthusiasm".

You've got to have enthusiasm: if your heart's not in it – give it away. I look for passion, flexibility and excitement. I try to employ enthusiastic people: people who aren't brain dead.

Walking the talk: We made Column 8 in the Sydney Morning Herald because I put an ad in the paper that read like this: Wanted: Manager, with hands-on experience and passion.

Column 8 wrote: "Hey, this guy's looking for trouble!"

14. SACRED COWS

We get so comfortable because we put everything in the same spot every day. Our lives and our businesses are full of sacred cows.

My staff love to put the product in the same place every day, because it's easy and efficient – so I make them move it around. I want them to break that pattern.

Make your customers move their eyes around your stock. A regular customer will say: "Where's your French Sticks today?" They won't see it because the French Sticks have been moved somewhere else, and they have to search for it, and while they're doing that they'll see something else they didn't know you stocked. They'll say: "Oh, you sell pumpkin bread too, I'll have one of them as well."

At the dinner table my son Peter likes the top seat. So I'll jump in first and he'll get so upset that he can hardly eat his dinner! "That's my chair Dad, you're sitting in my chair!" It's bloody sacred to him!

We get our sacred chairs in our houses.

"This is where I sit and watch TV

This is my side of the bed

This is my chair"

This is bullshit!

Where do they learn this from?

Even when he was three-years-old my little Matthew was saying: "This is my seat, Daddy this is my seat!"

Well, I like to pinch their seat.

You should see how upset they get!

The only seat I'm not game enough to pinch is Christine's. She sits in the same seat every time because she can't see any sense in having everybody upset at the dinner table.

15. OCCASIONALLY TELL YOUR BOSS TO GET STUFFED

I know some of my staff are a bit afraid of me, I'm not the most predictable person in the world. They say: "Shit! What's that bugger going to do next?"

I don't want my staff to be scared of me.

On the other hand, some of them aren't scared at all. They tell me to "get stuffed" and to "get out of the bloody way". I fire up and give as good as I get.

I sometimes yell at my manager. Then he'll yell back, and I'll yell at him some more and say: "Why don't you bloody yell at some of the staff like that?"

And he'll say: "Because they don't misbehave like you!"

Walking the talk: I don't rip people's heads off much today because then I've got to go back and apologise. I hate saying sorry. I hate it!

But I have to.

And sometimes I've got to apologise in my newsletter, I've got to say: "I'm sorry for trying to stick Linda in the oven, I was wrong."

16. SUPPORT YOUR COMMUNITY

We try to support our community in every way we can. We do it because it's good for others, it's good for Beechworth and it's good for our reputation. We freeze our food down at the end of every working day – which is a pain in the bum because we have to carry the freezer space – and we give the product to disadvantaged groups, single mums, needy people, the prison and the prisoners' families on special occasions, like Father's Day. The prisoners look after us; we've never been broken into yet. When they get out of prison, they cash their cheque at the Bakery.

Yes, we do lots of things, but we don't let other people sell our product. We don't do any wholesaling.

Walking the talk: The Bakery has tried all sorts of things to entertain and support the community. We used to have a courtyard where we built a miniature replica of Ned Kelly's hut for the kids to play in. We put bottomless cups of tea and coffee in our shop –

people love it. We lent one of the baker figurines from our window to the Gay & Lesbian Travel Show. They dressed him in black rubber and he was quite something!

17. YOU CAN'T BEAT CASH

Our business is totally cash, if somebody wants 20 per cent discount, I want to cut out 20 per cent of the ingredients – and it doesn't taste real good, I can tell you.

Walking the talk: I like cash. But these days EFTPOS is a big part of our business.

18. GET THEM TO BEECHWORTH

When I get on radio and television, I don't invite people to come to my bakery – I invite them to come to Beechworth, because I know that once they're here it's good for the whole town, and some of it will rub off on us. In this way, if you support your community, you'll always do well.

If I can get them to Beechworth I've got a chance of getting a dollar out of their pockets – but first I've got to get them here.

So I promote the town all the time, "Beechworth, Beechworth, gotta get them to Beechworth!" And they come! It still shocks me silly when I look at all these people coming to our town. I just keep inviting the people – I tell them we're famous. You tell them often enough and they'll believe you. It's so simple – just keep inviting them.

Walking the talk: Look at Beechworth today. It's a hive of activity. But when I came to town in 1984, these shops were all boarded up. The Scottish Shop wasn't there, the Provender wasn't there, the Bank Restaurant wasn't there, the Emporium wasn't there, the Lolly Shop wasn't there, the Ice Creamery wasn't there, the Alpaca Shop wasn't there, Beechworth Boudoir wasn't there, Mike's Bazaar wasn't there, Bridge Road Brewery wasn't there, Warden's

Restaurant wasn't there, the Pottery Shop wasn't there – I could go on and on. Wow! R M Williams wasn't there. Beechworth Pantry wasn't there. Lots of these businesses didn't exist.

In those days, if there was a car parked in the main street on a Sunday morning, everybody was wondering who got locked up or who got laid. Today, you're lucky if you can get a park.

19. IF YOU WOULDN'T BUY IT, DON'T SELL IT

I tell all my staff, if you wouldn't buy it, don't sell it. And then the bastards take me at my word! I'll come into the bakery and they'll be chucking all this stuff in the bin and I'll be going: "I'd sell it! I'd cut off the bloody burned bits! I'd ice over it!" But they're throwing it out! And I'm thinking, aah shit what did I say that for?

And then I'll go home.

Every one of my staff is empowered by this rule: if they wouldn't buy it themselves, they're not to sell it. So that guarantees every customer gets a good product.

I'll say to my bakers: "Would you want your mother to buy that?" And they'll say "no" and I'll say: "Bloody hell, then don't expect anyone else's mother to buy it!" I'll scream: "Do you reckon that's worth $3? Would you pay $3 for that?" I get a bit excited. And when my eyes start popping out of my head, most of them aren't game to get excited back.

Walking the talk: Any time I am angry, I tell my staff, it's not with them, it's with myself because I haven't communicated clearly. (That makes them feel much better.)

20. PROBLEMS ARE ALWAYS WITHIN MY FOUR WALLS

I'll sometimes sit in on our management meetings and say, "Our figures aren't going any good" and the staff will try to explain by saying, 'The weather has been too hot' or 'The people aren't around', 'Petrol is too dear!' or 'Tourist buses aren't coming in' or

'The bloody roadworks have interfered with the parking' or 'The supermarket's selling bread at $1.00 a loaf'"

and I'll say: "Bullshit!

Bullshit!

Bullshit!

It is not the supermarket, it is not the bloody weather, it's not the bloody buses!"

Any time I've got a problem with my business it's always within my four walls. It's not out there,

it's not the Council,

it's not the Government,

it's not the weather,

it's not the taxation system.

If I want to find the biggest problem in my business, all I've got to do is look in the mirror.

Walking the talk: If you've got problems with the supermarket, you can always pip them on quality. If you've got a problem with the heat, start making salads - stop making the bloody pies. If the tourist buses aren't coming in, send the staff home or send them on holidays. Cut down your labour – because that's my biggest cost.

Anytime I've got problems in my business, it's always within my four walls. Yet it's so easy to put the blame elsewhere. I've done it many times myself because I don't want to be responsible; I'd rather point the finger at somebody else. If I ever want to find the biggest problem in my business, all I've got to do is look in the mirror and I'll find the biggest problem I ever want to work with staring me in the face.

21. WHAT IF YOU TRAIN THEM AND THEY LEAVE?

The Beechworth Bakery spends a lot of money training its staff. We send them to seminars; we send them to work in other bakeries in other states and even overseas. Some people think we invest too much in my people and they say to me: "Tom, what if you train them and they leave?"

To which I usually reply: "What if I don't and they stay!"

Walking the talk: We put a lot of money into training courses for our staff, supervisors and managers.

As I've said before: The more you learn, the more you earn.

22. NO DISCOUNTS

We don't sell yesterday's product. We don't do Daily Specials or anything like that. We don't do any discounting. I don't sell day-old bread for 50 cents. People say, "Why don't you?" I say, "Because I haven't got a secondhand licence."

I never cut my prices at the end of the day. There are no discounts at the Beechworth Bakery, I prefer to chuck product out or give it to a needy cause.

Years ago I used to cut the prices at closing time, and at 7 pm when we'd be shutting I'd have all these bloody people in the doorway because everything was cheap. Some of these people wanted to buy big flour bags full of bread. So I started to stomp on the bread: "You want a bag of bread, here you are," and I'd jump on it, squash it up and hand it to them. That soon stopped them.

Walking the talk: We keep a good selection til the end of the day, because I want customers all day, until 7.00 pm closing time.

23. MY CUSTOMERS TELL ME HOW TO RUN MY BUSINESS

I've got 'Customer Comments' boxes spread throughout the shop because I believe the simplest way to run the business is to ask the customer what he or she wants. It's like having a free consultancy service working for you full time. I pin up some of the comments on the public noticeboard, the bad as well as the good. We get an average of 50 a week and we answer every one.

We get different types of comments and to many we've only got to write: "Thank you, thank you, thank you." But at times we do stuff up and we will get Mrs Jones writing, "I'm never coming to your shop again because I wasn't happy" and we have to write an apology. Plus we include some Beechworth Bakery dollars. A big problem is people's expectation of the Beechworth Bakery is so high, so at times they are let down – because our business is run by people.

But the customer isn't always right. The way some people find fault, you'd think there was a reward. I can't please everyone so sometimes I have to say "Go somewhere else". You can waste so much energy trying to please the one person who you're never going to please. I'm better off looking after the 98 per cent of the people who are happy coming into my business.

I've had other bakers say to me: "We put in a Customer Comments box and they told us to do this, and to do that and oh they whinged about everything, so we cut the comments out!" I think that's shooting the messenger.

However, I appreciate what my customers write even when they are critical of some aspect of the bakery. Customers write and tell us how to run the business better, and we try to take their advice.

I've got to be careful though, because they'd have us selling hot chips, fried chickens and ice creams, and I have to stay focused.

Walking the talk: In the early days, I was under the perception that we couldn't grow any more. We were turning over about $1.5 million a year. If you're turning over that sort of money across a bakery counter in Australia, you're doing pretty good. Then I stuck these Customer Comment boxes in and they told me how to do it better, and the Beechworth Bakery more than doubled that turnover figure!

24. TOILET TALK

I thought I couldn't do it any better, but geez the Customer Comments told me how to! They told me to put seats upstairs: my business started to pick up.

Now the dream-takers told me the opposite: "Upstairs is nil value – especially in rural Australia. You will not get people upstairs Tom. You can't even rent the space." I listened to these dream-takers for quite a while, but the customers kept writing in – we want more room! We want more room! I thought, how do I get them there? So we put in the toilets, that soon got the buggers upstairs.

We stuck in two toilets – out of the goodness of our heart – because we're a bakery, not a restaurant. Two toilets, and the customers kept on writing in: want more toilets! Want more toilets!

I exclaimed: "There's no money in bloody toilets! The amount of toilet paper them ladies use is ridiculous!" But we ended up putting in four more; we also have babies change tables in both the male and the female rest rooms. The people love it and today, every week, we get at least one comment: "Love your toilets".

Walking the talk: I've seen the opposite in lots of businesses, even here in Beechworth on one of the hotel doors - the sign reads: "Toilets are for patrons only."

Well, in our place you don't have to buy anything to use them they're for everybody. Toilets are a drawcard.

25. KING OF KIDS!

We show lots of school groups through the bakery. The kids come in and the staff look after them. I used to do that job, but once I got out of the bakery my production manager said to Christine: "Tell Tom we're cutting out the school groups" but I wouldn't let them.

Again, I'd never communicated to my staff why the kids were so important. They just thought I liked being King of the Kids, but there were far deeper reasons.

The greatest asset that any community or any business can have is its kids, they're its future. Today my staff look after the school kids. The kids all make a biscuit – they decorate it – then they make a loaf of bread which we bake for them and it's their bakery. They take that loaf home and Dad's got to take some to work, grandma's got to have a bit, Mum's got to have a taste. Next time Mum goes to buy bread in Albury, the kids will say: "Let's go to the Beechworth Bakery!"

That other guy, he had 12 apostles, but I have hundreds of the little buggers preaching the word of the Beechworth Bakery. Some of them are now six foot tall, and they eat like a bloody horse! Lots of the kids who visited the bakery are now married. They've got kids of their own. It's incredible how they breed.

It's a pain in the bum taking school groups through. It messes up production, but I'll tell you what, it's taught my bakers a lot of self-esteem,

it's taught them to talk to groups

it's taught them to be proud of their jobs.

It makes their jobs braggable.

These kids look up to our bakers!

Walking the talk: The Beechworth Bakery offers apprenticeships – and local kids can get part-time work at the bakery. My father-in-law Steve has got a chance to see his grandkids going to school in Beechworth and hopefully get a job here instead of having to go off to the city like many other rural kids in towns with shrinking populations and shrinking employment opportunities.

26. BE FRESH

Some bakers say to me: "Tom, our product's better than yours!" (They might be turning over $600,000 or, if they're real lucky, they might be turning over $1 million.) But their product is so good they keep it for two days after they should have got rid of it – whereas my staff are all empowered: if they wouldn't buy it they're not to sell it. So they keep it fresh.

Some of these bakers do such beautiful work. They say, "Tom, our product leaves yours for dead" – but we're the one turning over $3.2 million and they're the ones turning over $600,000. (Though, I tell you what, you can make a good living on their turnover figure – though you'd have to be in there working – because it isn't big enough to have a manager and a lifestyle.)

Some bakers volunteer to work in our bakery because they want to find out the secret of our success.

They come all the way from other states, and sometimes other countries, which is a big effort just to learn to keep everything fresh. But I don't care what they find out - it's free labour for me and they get a big mind-expanding experience.

Walking the talk: We send our bakers to work in other bakeries too. I get on well with other bakers because I've got nothing to hide.

27. THE WORLD'S GREATEST BAKERY?

A few years ago we had a bakery open up across the road and everyone said: "Tom, aren't you worried?" Naaah! As I said, there's a lot of customers that you can't bloody please, they whinge and moan and bitch no matter what you do. So when I got a customer comment like that, I wrote back, gave them my competitor's business card and told them to go across the road. He got all the whingers and moaners and went broke in no time.

Some bakers say, "Tom, who says you're Australia's Greatest Bakery?" Well, I get out of the question by showing them a couple of Customer Comments – because a lot of our customers write: 'You're Australia's greatest bakery." Some even write: "You're the world's greatest bakery!"

That's a pretty big boast, "Australia's Greatest Bakery" but as far as we know, we have the greatest sales for any stand-alone retail bakery in Australia (no wholesale).

And we genuinely try to make the Bakery great. Business has got to be fun. I ask people: "Are you allowed to make mistakes? Are you allowed to take risks? Have you got a future? Would you like your kids working in your business?" And I've got to ask myself that too: "Would I like my kids working in my business? Is it happy? Is it crazy? Are we allowed to take risks?" Yep, we are!

28. CHOOSE TO BE HAPPY

The power of choice is incredible. We can choose to think great thoughts, we can choose enthusiasm, we can choose to bungee jump right out of our comfort zones. Because I've never used a calculator or a computer, I used to say, "I can't use a calculator, I can't use a computer"; today I say, "I choose not to", and there's a world of difference in that wording.

However, I'm a bit of a liar because programmed into my laptop are the slides I use for presentations. It's much easier than carrying those old carousels. But these days I feel a bit besieged with emails, text messages, Facebook and everything.

Still, I don't let them rule my life. I don't get tied up with emails, I get Christine to handle them. However, I do write blogs every few days, again with a lot of help from Christine. Although I find technology a real pain, it's all about change. I have to be open to new things. If you finish learning, you're buggered.

We all have choices (what we do with our time, what we put into our heads, whether or not to be up with the times) so choose to be happy. Abe Lincoln said: "Most people are as happy as they make up their mind to be." When we get out of bed in the morning we have two choices – either to be happy or unhappy. So many buggers chose to be unhappy.

Your alarm clock is an opportunity clock. When it tells you to 'get out of bed', instead of staying there – get into life and get rarin' to go.

29. TELL ME WHAT I'M DOING RIGHT

I'm really good at telling people what they're doing wrong. I've got bloody laser vision. I'll come into the bakery and I'll see a speck in the showcase. I'll see a switch not turned on – and bloody hell, I'm warming up! Then I'll go into the bakehouse and I'll see they've burned a rack of pies, and I'll say, "Look at these! They're bloody burned! You pricks! What are you bloody doing?"

They can see that the pies are burned. They're feeling bad enough without me ripping their bloody heads off.

It does me no good telling the staff what they've done wrong, yet I think it does. I know they don't get out of bed in the morning and say: "Let's see what we can stuff up today". They don't do that. They want to do the best job.

All staff do, I believe.

Walking the talk: The message we should communicate is: don't tell me what I'm doing wrong, tell me what I'm doing right.

They do 99 things right and one thing wrong and I want to rip their bloody heads off. I must be crazy!

30. IT'S GOT TO BE SIMPLE

I believe everything has to be simple. That's why all through this book you kept reading the words, That's how bloody simple it is. If it's not simple – nobody's going to remember it, so nobody's going to do it.

Human nature has never changed. The best example of simplicity is the one I used in the previous chapter: that all customers want you to: look at them, greet them, talk to them, and thank them.

That's so simple, but we often don't do it. We can get so tied up in spreadsheets, flowcharts, databases and complicated stuff. Just look the customer in the eye and smile. Everyone smiles in the same language. It's that simple.

Walking the talk: I don't want to look at the buggers either, because they'll expect me to serve them if I give them that eye contact. Next point!

31. WHAT DO YOU THINK OF YOURSELF?

I used to sabotage myself because I was scared of success. I bought the nice cars, then I was too embarrassed to drive them. I was scared of success as well as being scared of failure. Often we think: "What will people think if we buy a Lexus?" or "What will people think if we get divorced?" The only thing that counts is what you think of yourself.

In some ways I'm very grateful I never learned the ABC. If I'd had a school education I probably wouldn't be where I am today. Today it gives me a uniqueness. I'm different.

Honestly, I feel a fraud in lots of areas. I've got such mixed feelings: on one hand here I am writing out my 'philosophies' knowing deep down that I'm no bloody big time guru; yet on the other hand I know that the success of the Beechworth Bakery can't be just luck.

I was already successful at the Ideal Café all those years ago. It was bursting at the seams when we sold it. And in Augusta I built up another very good business, so I must have some skills. I also have great enthusiasm. I'm in love with life and rarin' to go. I'm enthusiastic about work, I'm enthusiastic about sweeping the floor. If I'm cleaning the trays, I'm enthusiastic! I suppose I learned that off my Dad. He was a great worker. He'd be pushing the carts around the railway station, singing the whole time. And that is probably a real blessing, because enthusiasm is like measles and mumps – highly contagious. If you aren't getting what you want out of life, check your level of enthusiasm.

Walking the talk: Nothing worthwhile is ever achieved without that collective spark of enthusiasm.

Here's a poem by my big sister Betty, it's called:

TOM'S ADVICE

Don't listen to the dream-takers
When they tell you what to do
For what may seem just right for them
May not be right for you
We may all be wrong, misjudging the path
We may even suffer some pain
But when you make a mistake yourself
Get up and try again.

Don't let others put you down
Make you guilty or afraid
For if you let them gain control
You'll end up as their slave
So be honest and fair-hearted
Independent, free and true
Although you'll sometimes get it wrong
That's always up to you.

Others are not perfect
No better than you are
They'll find that hard to understand
If you follow your own star
So keep your eye upon your God
Whatever your God may be

```
Steer your own eternal course
      Fulfil your destiny.
```

Thanks Betty.

THE END

So now I've told you all about myself, my life and my key philosophies.

I know I couldn't have done it without Christine, because she gives me a lot of stability. I also know I couldn't have done it without lots of people, many of whom are on my payroll, and many who haven't been mentioned in the book.

As for you, the reader, I've given you my best shot. I haven't got any secrets.

And if you've just read everything I've written and you're carelessly fiddling with a calculator watch instead of being in love with life and rarin' to go – watch out –

I'll jump right out of this book,

grab you by the neck

and I'll try to stick you in the bloody oven!

BREADWINNER

THE BEECHWORTH BAKERY

From November 1852, up to 9000 miners surged to the area. In 1852 the Gold Commissioner's camp was established on the northern banks of the Spring Creek stream. This consolidated the area as a centre. The government officers chose terrain which was high enough for them to overlook the diggings on the other side of the creek, yet safe enough from marauding miners. This government area was order and authority, while the miners' area was shifting, uncertain scatterings of habitation.

Initially, the commissioners had to rough it in tents like the miners. But there was no way they lived in shambles. Sentries stood on duty as in a military camp. A bell suspended to the flagstaff of the large central Court House Tent rang out the hours. There were tents for servants, tents for officers, a Police Court tent and a Camp Hospital tent. The Commissioner's camp was soon joined on the granite knoll by the shop and hotels of Beechworth's future businessmen.

The current address of the Beechworth Bakery, at 27 Camp Street, goes back to 1853 when Surveyor Smythe marked roads, building allotments and reserves on a clear grid plan. A high granite area, known by pastoralists as The Sandy Forest, it was bordered on three sides by Spring Creek and its tributary Holmes Creek.

Before this date, the townsfolk could obtain no legal tenure on their land. Five months after the first gold was taken out, storekeepers anxious to consolidate their trade sent a deputation to the government requesting the township be surveyed. Prospective buyers gathered for the auction at the Beechworth Police Office on 7 September 1853. Some storekeepers were already squatting on the sites they wanted to buy. And no one contested them. Forty-four one-quarter acre township lots and six suburban lots were auctioned, the site of the Beechworth Bakery among them.

ORIGINAL OWNERSHIP OF LAND

The government gave local traders permission to build on the surveyed lots in Beechworth before the land was sold, with the assurance that the value of improvements would be added to the reserve price of the land. (In case someone other than the current occupiers purchased the land at the land sales.)

Between March and June 1853, Charles Williams erected a large store (at a cost of 400 pounds) on Lots 1 and 20 of Camp Street, which included the Beechworth Bakery site. It is not known whether this first store occupied the whole of Lots 1 and 20 or whether the store occupied the actual site of the present bakery. "My guess is that it did, as Charles Williams' store would almost certainly have been at the Ford Street end of the block," says local historian, Ian Hyndman.

The first land sales took place on 7 September 1853, at which Williams was successful in officially purchasing these blocks. Charles Williams was therefore the first person to erect a store on the site.

Williams arrived at Beechworth from Tasmania in 1852. He was a lay preacher in the Methodist Church in the early years when services were held in a tent. He was elected as a member of the first Municipal Council in Beechworth in 1856.

The municipal district of Beechworth was proclaimed on 23 August 1856.

Land prices soared, new subdivisions were eagerly snapped up. Timber merchants, brickmakers and quarriers supplied the rush to build. Artisans were sought to do the very best work. Substantial buildings remain more than 140 years later as testament to the excellent standard of construction. The best materials were hauled to the town. Beechworth was shaping up to be a major centre in the north east of Victoria.

GENERAL STORE

The original Lot 1-20 is where Beechworth Bakery is found today, and it originally reached to the Ford and Camp Street corner. On a lithographed map from the Surveyor General's Office dated 17 October 1856, it appears a G Black purchased this land from Williams. There is mention of a George Black, a miner, who made an impassioned speech at a rally in early 1853 against the gold licence tax system. "While valuing the miners' position as Britons and wanting to support all constituted authorities, there was a point to which their forbearance should not be stretched," he said. A petition was signed and sent to Governor Latrobe who agreed to look into the matter. The miners and the government officials rarely saw life through the same eyes. Storekeepers and miners alike thought the government camp was full of arrogant, insensitive characters. The government camp deliberately isolated itself from the miners' and the shopkeepers' areas.

Within nine months of this map being produced the first documented owner of the 27 Camp Street site where the Beechworth Bakery now stands was goldminer Fred Hill who, on 9 July 1857, purchased the land. The price was 187 pounds and 10 shillings. Fresh gold finds dwindled until 1855 but then improved gold prospects caused a town-land boom. Hill bought during this boom.

About 120 business people, including publicans, were involved in the sale of food and drink in Beechworth in 1857. William Thompson Soulby, was among them and would inherit the bakery premises 30 years later. In 1857, Soulby owned the Victoria Hotel and Dining Rooms in High Street. He was aiming for a certain 'high class' standard, and got it. In 1859, he built in Camp Street his brick and stone London Tavern and added two extra wings in 1861-62. He opened St George's Hall in Camp Street in 1866. Famous entertainers performed here – like Walter Montgomery, General Tom Thumb and three other dwarves.

In the time of Hill's brief ownership of the property, the only bakers in Camp Street were: Scott & Morriss, Merchants and Bakers, and E Ansell & Hazelton, Bakers.

A lithograph of the block where the Beechworth Bakery now stands shows it was bound by a picket fence. Across the road, the Post Office is a neat, verandah-clad timber building as are all adjacent buildings. Next door to the Post Office is James Ingram's Stationers and Bookshop. The look of order is apparent. The new stores are well stocked and clean. Gone are the wood, bark and canvas shelters initially flung together to service miners. The town, estimated to number more than 3000, was shaping up very differently to the diggings just down the road.

Conditions at the diggings were very rough and arduous. Leaning over his picket fence and looking down the length of Camp Street towards Spring Creek, Fred Hill would have seen thousands of miners. Sweat-soaked men were sluicing through the mud, digging, carting and hauling. Few newcomers knew each other. Murders and deaths were frequent. Trees were ripped up for fuel or to mark claims. Flies were everywhere. Insects crawled over everything. The heat in summer was intense. There was no sanitation. No disposal of waste and rubbish. Dysentry and infections were common.

SHOEMAKER

Fred Hill did not hang on to the land for long. Within six months he sold it to boot and shoemaker William Glover. (During renovations, Tom found lots of leather offcuts under the floorboards.) On 3 December 1857, Hill made a profit of 12 pounds and 10 shillings. The selling price was 200 pounds.

Glover remained the owner for many years. In the rate book for 1861 there is mention of a 'deal and glass-fronted shop with slabs and shingle and some weatherboarding'.

Eleven years after the initial purchase, Glover needed cash. He arranged a mortgage through John Trahair, a successful local miner originally from St Just, Cornwall. The terms of the mortgage were 300 pounds to be repaid with interest after three years. Glover never reached the end of the mortgage term because he decided to sell his mortgaged land within a year of the contract.

Glover would have seen the granite walls of the Beechworth Gaol go up. He would have witnessed the terrible fire that destroyed much of the other side of Camp Street in 1867. The heat was so intense that the Bakery side of the street was under threat. Glover would have known Robert O'Hara Burke. Burke, later to die with Wills in an ill-fated expedition in 1861, was known around Beechworth as having a poor sense of direction when venturing into the bush.

In 1866, David Dunlop, a pastrycook, is noted in the rate book along with William Glover. Perhaps this future purchaser of the property was sharing the site with the bootmaker.

BAKERY

What is definite is that on 24 February 1869, Glover sold to Dunlop for 200 pounds and it appears Dunlop took on the terms of the existing mortgage with Trahair. In effect, the land sold for 500 pounds (200 cash plus 300 mortgage and the interest). David Dunlop was the first baker to own the site.

He paid out the mortgage on 28 June 1871. In a sense, 28 June celebrates when the Beechworth Bakery was first owned by a baker. It is, therefore, David Dunlop Day. Dunlop was elected to the Beechworth Municipal Council in 1876.

Shoppers in Beechworth increasingly consisted of townspeople rather than customers drawn from the surrounding diggings, and those diggers who did shop were more subdued than their counterparts of the 1850s.

On Saturday nights the shops remained open till 10 pm. There was no rowdiness or drunkenness. Bookshops were popular.

During the 1870s a steady stream of members of the Kelly family, relatives and associates appeared before the Beechworth Courts.

Dunlop may have noticed Ned Kelly walk past on his way to having his portrait taken in the studios of James Bray in Camp Street. He wore a suit and double-breasted waistcoat. James Ingram recalls Ned visiting his book shop and describes him thus: "He was in his usual manner, of a quiet, unassuming disposition, a polite and gentlemanly man."

When just 19, in August, 1874, Ned Kelly won an unofficial heavyweight boxing match against Wild Wright. It was 20 rounds of bare knuckle fighting and it happened in Beechworth below the Imperial Hotel in High Street.

But such observations turned to more frightening stories. This was the era of the rise of the Kelly Gang. Beechworth became central to the saga. On 26 June 1880, Aaron Sherritt was murdered by Joe

Byrne, who was killed with Dan Kelly two days later at the siege at Glenrowan. And on 1 August 1880, Ned Kelly was transported from Beechworth Gaol to Melbourne after being arrested at Glenrowan. It was a Sunday afternoon when the train pulled in and 100 people gathered to see him arrive.

Just over three months later Ned Kelly was hanged in Melbourne Gaol. Today, his death mask, reproductions of his armour, and as much about his life as can possibly fit into one museum corner, is on display at Beechworth's Burke Museum.

Dunlop died on 10 June 1887. His wife survived him only for nine months. The Beechworth Bakery site, according to her will, was to be sold and the proceeds given to the heirs. Soulby was one to inherit but he "renounced probate of the will". This left the other heir, James Morrison McMaster of Beechworth, a baker, to claim the lot. One condition of the will was that the premises be sold. So James had his wife Rosina, a woman of independent means, buy the property from him.

BAKERY

On 31 December 1888, Rosina McMaster bought the site for 500 pounds.

The 1889 rate book shows a shop, dwelling and premises were on the site. Rosina retained the premises for many years but needed to raise some capital. Trahair was again approached to arrange a mortgage. After Trahair's death in early 20th century, this contract with Rosina was noted. His heirs continued to do business with Rosina.

At least four times in the brief history of this site the property has been mortgaged to John Trahair and his heirs.

(It is interesting to note that Trahair lived on five acres at Silver Creek when he retired. Tom and Christine also live at Silver Creek.)

Thirty-three years after purchasing the site, Rosina McMaster sold to James Clingin of Beechworth for 600 pounds in April 1922.

In this period, prominent Beechworth businessman and Kelly raconteur, James Ingram, died on 28 March 1928, just six weeks short of his 100th birthday. The business premises opposite the Bakery still bear his name.

BAKERY

On 24 April 1922, James Clingin took out a mortgage on 27 Camp Street with the Beechworth Building Society for 480 pounds.

This mortgage between Clingin and the Beechworth Building Society was paid in full on 10 September 1930.

TEA ROOMS

Clingin agreed to sell the land to Matthew Byrne in 1926 for 1200 pounds. But Byrne only paid 500 pounds; he never paid off the rest of his debt. Clingin was a partner in the business.

It was called Byrne's Tea Rooms and described as, "Best kinds of confectionary. Meals and light refreshments at all hours. Agents for Adams' famous cakes". It was still an agency for Adam's Cakes when Tom first bought it in 1974.

Byrne was a fruiterer and confectioner who died on 7 May 1931, and his widow Annie was the executor of his will. Annie paid all her husband's debts including the 700 pounds owing to Clingin who moved to Preston, Melbourne, in 1933.

CONFECTIONARY SHOP

On 9 October 1935, Annie Byrne sold to Elisha Gribble and his wife Elizabeth, confectioners, formerly of Beechworth, for 1500 pounds.

CAFÉ

The Gribbles moved to Moonee Ponds and they sold to café proprietor James Pooley for 556 pounds, on 7 February 1947, for a fraction of what they paid for it 12 years earlier.

PASTRYSHOP

On 3 September 1948 Pooley sold to pastrycook Stanley Smyth and his wife Margaret for 710 pounds.

During this period, Beechworth was a forlorn historical monument in the north-east divested of all facets of its former glory.

The Beechworth Mining Board, along with other mining boards in Victoria, had been phased out in 1914. Supreme Court sittings were moved from Beechworth to Wangaratta in 1918, and Beechworth lost the Courts of General Sessions in 1943. The tannery closed in 1961, and other factories also closed, ending all hopes for an industrial base. The last train from Wangaratta ran in December 1976.

THE IDEAL CAFÉ

Smyth held the land and leased the premises until Tom O'Toole, Betty and Allan Friar purchased the site from him in 1974. In 1964 Betty Kent and her partner Kelvin Hill struggled to make the business work. Betty was extremely industrious and when she took over the business she worked it for four and a half years turned it around until she sold it as a viable business to Keith and Bernie McIntosh. In 1974 they sold the Ideal Café business to Tom, Betty and Allan for $27,000.

In 1977 Tom, Betty and Allan sold the freehold and the business to boxers Johnny van Gorkom and John Holt for $110,000.

THE BEECHWORTH BAKERY

Tom O'Toole purchased the Ideal Café in 1984 for $110,000 and changed its name to the Beechworth Bakery, after which – it was all the way to the top. Tom also bought the building next door. In 2001 the name was so well established that it was retained when Tom opened a second bakery known as Beechworth Bakery Echuca.

BREAD

"All men at God's round table sit
And all men must be fed
But this loaf in my hand
This loaf is my son's bread"
Mary Gilmore, Nationality

The history of bread goes way back. They say baking is the second-oldest profession. And it's true, bakeries have been around a long time. Other professions come and go as technology changes, but the baker has survived.

In Australia, the history of old money is a history of the flour mills. Every regional centre had its four-storey flour mill, which supplied all the local bakers. The late '50s marked the first of three revolutions in bread-making techniques. Before the '50s the doughs were hand-made. Starting up one end of a table 12 feet long, each local baker would knead the dough by hand. Because of this, many bakers contracted emphysema inhaling flour dust – a disease from which their sons were spared through the advent of machine-made doughs, all with the strictest of quality controls. The new improved machinery of the 1950s-60s ensured that the baker could bake more quality as well as quantity, a better, more standardised loaf.

The new breed of bakers ceased to be craftsmen. Supermarket bread had arrived and the independent flour mills were being bought up and turned into subsidiaries of the giants. The individualism was going out of the humble loaf.

In late 1957, Albury-based Bunge Australia decided to diversify from being a flour miller only, and it moved into owning and operating bakeries. Sunicrust Bakery was formed and in 1958 the first bakery was purchased at Ballarat. Between 1958-63, it bought 10 bakeries, mostly in Victoria, including Wangaratta, Albury and Wodonga. From 1964-1968 many bakeries were acquired as a result of them being in debt to the flour mills. Some were rationalised and some now form the base network for the very successful Sunicrust organisation.

In 1966, in an attempt to protect local bakers from corporate competitors, legislation was passed in Victoria which allowed bakeries to service within a 30 mile (48 km) radius only of the bakery. In 1968 Tom O'Toole commenced his apprenticeship in Tocumwal.

North eastern Victoria's bakeries were subject to buy-outs nevertheless. It was a struggle between Sunicrust and Sunwise, and Sunicrust chose to move into the Melbourne metropolitan area where it concentrated on servicing a denser population, in fact within a 30 mile radius. While Sunwise was buying up the flour mills and winding down the bakeries, Sunicrust concentrated its efforts on Melbourne until 1972.

Tom returned from Maningrida only to find Sunicrust reactivating its country interests. Its first major acquisition was the 12 flour mills and bakeries of Sunwise which included Cobram, Shepparton and Wangaratta, where Tom had previously worked. Tom then bought a bakery at Yarrawonga. From 1972-79 the list of acquisitions goes on, with fingers stretching into south New South

Wales and south eastern Victoria. Sunicrust is now the largest volume bakery of plant bread in Victoria, and is growing its aggressive policy of strategic acquisitions and market share growth.

However, in 1974 a significant niche became apparent when Hades Hot Bread initiated the doomed franchise in south Victoria. The owner exported the idea and became successful in Great Britain, but in Warragul he was before his time as evidenced by the rise of hot bread shops since.

In 1975, the first Old Style Bakery Centre (OSBC) opened in the Melbourne suburb, Ashburton, then opening in Brisbane (1981) and undergoing a major structural change. In 1983, OSBC opened its first franchised store in Moorabin. In 1985, OSBC became Brumby's which continued its rapid franchise growth. There are currently more than 250 Brumby's hot bread shops in Australia and New Zealand.

However, Brumby's is not Australia's largest group of franchised bakeries; that crown goes to Baker's Delight, which started in 1980 and has over 550 stores. Tom could have followed the pattern and opened just another hot bread shop or a patisserie – another niche market that has blossomed under the mega-centralisation of regional flour mills and local bakeries.

But, instead, the Beechworth Bakery has followed a completely different path, with 250 lines, musical bands, regular events and a constant stream of innovative changes. Instead of succumbing to centralisation, the Beechworth Bakery has become a centre in itself.

More Tom O'Toole Inspirational Products

DVD - Making Dough & Tom the Speaker

Visit Tom and his staff on the job at the Beechworth Bakery and hear their take on business & life.

Presented in two parts, part one is a fascinating & witty 15 minutes of ideas, practices and recipes on business success the Beechworth Bakery way.

Part two features Tom live on stage in his capacity as one of Australia's leading inspirational speakers.

Comes with a complimentary copy of *Breadwinner*.

Price: **$198**

DVD - Drop Everything for the Customer

Customer Service the Beechworth Bakery way

This is an inspirational guide for any-sized business, exploring 'the secret' that made the Beechworth Bakery what it is today.

Presented in four bite-sized sections, Tom's methods, ideas and advice are practical and simple to implement. Observe Beechworth Bakery customer service in action and find out how to cultivate and grow this vital component in your business. Comes with a complimentary copy of *Breadwinner*.

Price: **$198**

DVD - Dare to Dream

How Setting Goals Can Grow Your Business and Change Your Life

Another inspirational guide from Tom O'Toole.

Let Tom show you how the simple task of setting goals for yourself can help to grow you business and also change your life.

Price: **$198**

Audio CD - Winning Ways

Getting honest about business with Tom O'Toole. Enjoy Tom at his best, in front of a live audience. Travel with Tom through an amazing kaleidoscope of experiences and tales about his life and the Beechworth Bakery, pick up plenty of practical tips and ideas that may help you to grow your business.

Price: **$29.95**

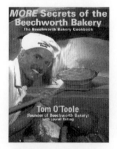

Book - More Secrets of the Beechworth Bakery

The Beechworth Bakery Cookbook

Peppered with passion and inspiration, this is the latest edition of the Beechworth Bakery's immensely popular collection of 'secrets', featuring even more recipes & snippets of wisdom, and challenging life's recipes.

Price: **$24.95**

To contact Tom O'Toole:
www.tomotoole.com.au
info@tomotoole.com.au
Phone: 03 5728 1339
Fax: 03 5728 3194